# Excel 5 for the Mac
## The Visual Learning Guide

1-2-3 for Windows: The Visual Learning Guide
WINDOWS Magazine Presents: Access from the Ground Up
Access from the Ground Up, 2nd Edition
Advanced PageMaker 4.0 for Windows
Adventures in Windows
CompuServe Information Manager for Windows: The Complete Handbook and Membership Kit
Create Wealth with Quicken
WINDOWS Magazine Presents: Encyclopedia for Windows
Excel 4 for Windows: Everything You Need to Know
Excel 4 for Windows: The Visual Learning Guide
Excel 5 for Windows: The Visual Learning Guide
Free Electronic Networks
WINDOWS Magazine Presents: Freelance Graphics for Windows: The Art of Presentation
Harvard Graphics for Windows: The Art of Presentation
Improv for Windows Revealed! (with 3½" disk)
LotusWorks 3: Everything You Need to Know
Microsoft Office In Concert
Microsoft Works for Windows By Example
PageMaker 4.0 for Windows: Everything You Need to Know
PageMaker 5.0 for Windows: Everything You Need to Know
PowerPoint: The Visual Learning Guide
WINDOWS Magazine Presents: The Power of Windows and DOS Together, 2nd Edition
Quattro Pro 4: Everything You Need to Know
Quicken 3 for Windows: The Visual Learning Guide
Smalltalk Programming for Windows (with 3½" disk)
Superbase Revealed!
SuperPaint 3: Everything You Need to Know
Think THINK C
Visual Basic for Applications Revealed!
Windows 3.1: The Visual Learning Guide
Windows for Teens
Word for Windows 2: The Visual Learning Guide
Word for Windows 2 Desktop Publishing By Example
Word for Windows 6: The Visual Learning Guide
WordPerfect 5.1 for Windows Desktop Publishing By Example
WordPerfect 6 for DOS: How Do I...?
WordPerfect 6 for Windows: The Visual Learning Guide
Your FoxPro for Windows Consultant (with 3½" disk)
WinFax PRO: The Visual Learning Guide
Lotus Notes Revealed!

**How to Order:**

Individual orders and quantity discounts are available from the publisher, Prima Publishing, P.O. Box 1260BK, Rocklin, CA 95677-1260; (916) 786-0426. For quantity orders, include information on your letterhead concerning the intended use of the books and the number of books you wish to purchase.

# Excel 5 for the Mac
## The Visual Learning Guide

Grace Joely Beatty, Ph.D.

David C. Gardner, Ph.D.

Prima Publishing
P.O. Box 1260BK
Rocklin, CA 95677-1260

Prima Computer Books is an imprint of Prima Publishing, Rocklin, California 95677.

Executive Editor: Roger Stewart
Managing Editor: Neweleen A. Trebnik
Acquisitions Editor: Sherri Morningstar
Project Editor: Andrew Mitchell
Cover Production Coordinator: Anne Johnson
Copyeditors: Becky Whitney and Kelley Mitchell
Technical Reviewer: Blue Moon Productions
Production: Craig A. Patchett
Indexer: Craig A. Patchett
Interior Design: Grace Joely Beatty, S. Linda Beatty, David C. Gardner,
   Laurie Stewart, and Kim Bartusch
Cover Design: Page Design, Inc.

ISBN: 1-55958-460-2
Library of Congress Card Number: 93-085781
Printed in the United States of America
95 96 97 98 RRD 10 9 8 7 6 5 4 3 2 1

# Acknowledgments

We are deeply indebted to reviewers around the country who gave generously of their time to test every step in the manuscript. David Coburn, Carolyn Holder, Ray Holder, David Sauer, Linda Miles, and Anne-Barbara Norris cannot be thanked enough!

Linda Beatty did all the work to translate this book into Mac-talk.

We are personally and professionally delighted to work with everyone at Prima Publishing, especially Roger Stewart, executive editor; Sherri Morningstar, acquisitions editor; Neweleen Trebnik, managing editor; Andrew Mitchell, project manager; Mike Van Mantgem, publicity coordinator; and Anne Johnson, cover coordinator.

Shawn Morningstar, our technical editor; Craig Patchett, who did the interior layout; and Paul Page, cover design, contributed immensely to the final product.

Bill Gladstone and Matt Wagner of Waterside Productions created the idea for this series. Their faith in us has never wavered.

Joseph and Shirley Beatty made this series possible. We can never repay them.

Asher Schapiro has always been there when we needed him.

Paula Gardner Capaldo and David Capaldo have been terrific. Thanks, Joshua and Jessica, for being such wonderful kids! Our project humorist, Mike Bumgardner, always came through when we needed a boost!

We could not have met the deadlines without the technical support of Ray Holder, our electrical genius; Diana M. Balelo, Frank E. Straw, Daniel W. Terhark, and Martin J. O'Keefe of Computer Service & Maintenance, our computer wizards.

# Contents at a Glance

# Customize
# Your Learning

Prima Visual Learning Guides are not like any other computer books you have ever seen. They are based on our years in the classroom, our corporate consulting, and our research at Boston University on the best ways to teach technical information to non-technical learners. Most important, this series is based on the feedback of a panel of reviewers from across the country who range in computer knowledge from "panicked at the thought" to very sophisticated.

This is not an everything-you've-ever-wanted-to-know-about-Excel 5 for the Macintosh book. It is designed to give you the information you need to perform all of the basic (and many advanced) functions with confidence and skill. It is a book that our reviewers claim makes it "really easy" for anyone to learn Excel 5 quickly.

Each chapter is illustrated with screen shots to guide you through every task. The combination of screens, step-by-step instructions, and pointers makes it impossible for you to get lost or confused as you follow along on your own computer. You can either work through from the beginning to the end or skip around to master skills you need.

We truly hope you'll enjoy using the book and the Excel program. Let us know how you feel about our book and if there are any changes/improvements we can make. You can contact us through Prima Publishing at the address on the title page. Thanks for choosing our book. Enjoy!

Joely and David

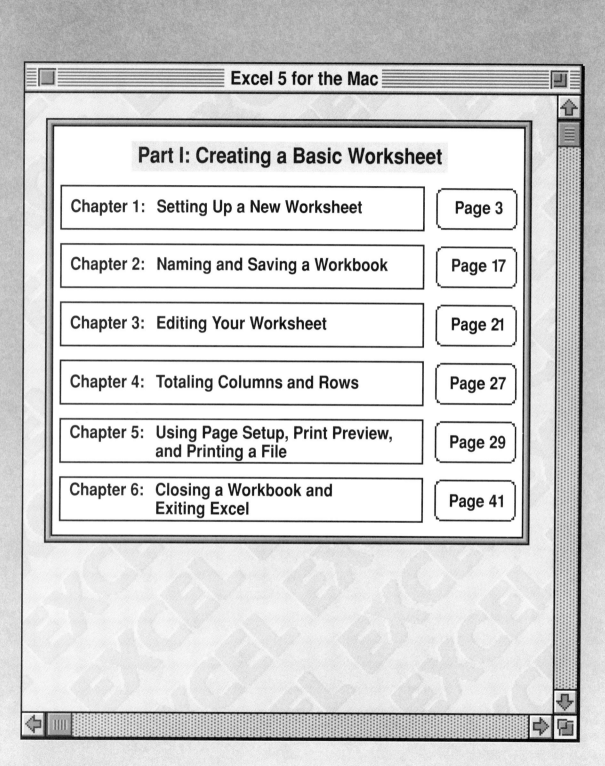

**Excel 5 for the Mac**

# Part I: Creating a Basic Worksheet

# Setting Up a New Worksheet

The latest version of Excel makes it especially easy to create a worksheet, format and manipulate data, and take advantage of new features.

In this chapter, you will do the following:

❖ Create a basic worksheet
❖ Complete a series
❖ Sort a column alphabetically

If you haven't installed Excel yet, turn to the Appendix, "Installing Excel 5."

## OPENING EXCEL

1. **Click twice** on the **hard drive icon** on your desktop. The hard drive folder will open. Because Macintosh provides for tremendous customization, you will probably have different icons on your screen.

If the Microsoft folder is already open, go to step 3 in this section.

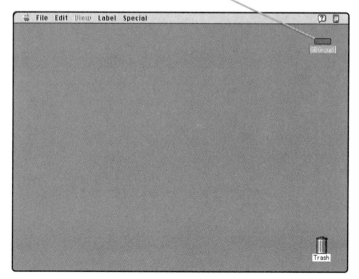

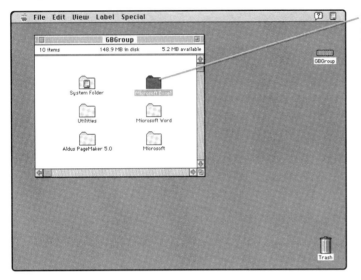

2. **Click twice** on the **Microsoft Excel folder.**

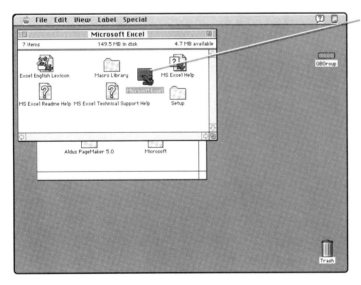

3. **Click twice** on the **Microsoft Excel icon.** You will see the copyright information for Excel, then the program will open and a new worksheet will appear.

# MAXIMIZING THE WORKSHEET

When you open (boot up) Excel for the first time, your screen may look like the example to the left. Notice that the worksheet does not fill the whole screen. You can change this very easily.

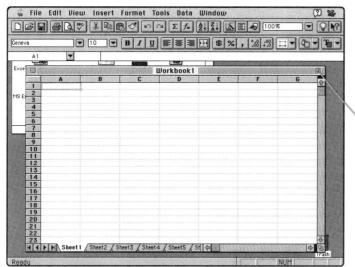

1. **Click** on the **Zoom box** on the right side of the Workbook 1 title bar. The worksheet will fill your screen.

# THE EXCEL WORKBOOK

Notice "Workbook1" in the title bar. The Excel work-book is the equivalent of a three-ring binder that holds multiple sheets and chart sheets.

Notice the tabs at the bottom of the workbook. You can have up to 255 sheets in a workbook. In Chapter 11, "Setting Up a Second Worksheet," you will put a name on the tab to identify the worksheet.

This is a close-up view of a portion of the screen. You will see both close-up views and full-screen views in this book.

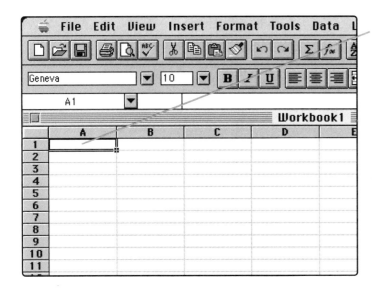

A worksheet is made up of *columns* and *rows*. The intersection of a column and a row forms a block, or *cell*. The *border* around the first cell on the worksheet tells you that this is the *active* cell. This is the cell that will be affected by the next entry or command.

Each cell has a unique *address,* or *reference.* The cell reference of the active cell shows in the Name box. The cell reference is A1 because the active cell is located in column A, row 1.

Notice the mouse pointer has a plus-sign shape when it is in the worksheet area. The pointer changes shape depending on its location and the action you are performing.

# ENTERING A WORKSHEET TITLE

When you create a worksheet, it is a good idea to enter a title. After the worksheet is printed, the worksheet title enables you (and others) to know the subject of the worksheet.

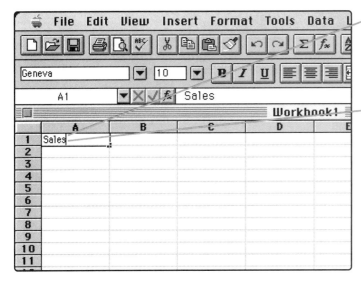

1. **Click** on cell **A1** if it does not already have a border around it. (On your screen, it will be blank.)

2. **Type** the word **Sales.** The letters will appear in the cell. They will also appear in the *contents box*, which displays characters as you type. If you make a typing error, just press the Delete key and retype.

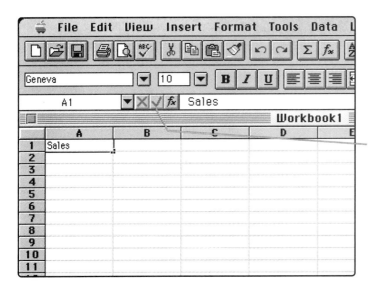

When you begin to type, notice that a red X (the *Cancel* button) and a green ✔ (the *Confirm* button) appear to the left of the contents box.

3. **Click** on the ✔ to confirm that you want to enter "Sales" into A1. The Cancel and Confirm buttons will disappear after you confirm the entry.

## ENTERING COLUMN HEADINGS

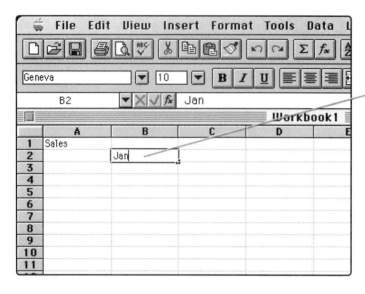

In this section, you will enter the abbreviation for January as the heading for column B.

1. **Click** on **B2.** On your screen, it will be blank.

2. **Type Jan.**

3. **Click** on the ✔ to confirm the entry.

## USING THE AUTOFILL FEATURE TO COMPLETE A SERIES

After you have typed the first name in a common series (such as months in the year or days in the week), you can use the AutoFill feature to complete the series.

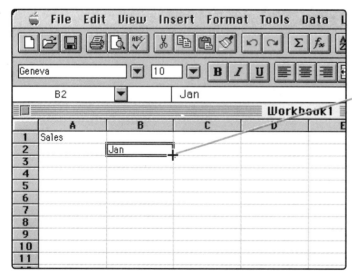

1. **Move** the mouse pointer **to the square** in the lower right corner of the cell. This square is called the *fill handle*. The pointer will change to a black plus sign. You may have to fiddle with the pointer to get it to change shape.

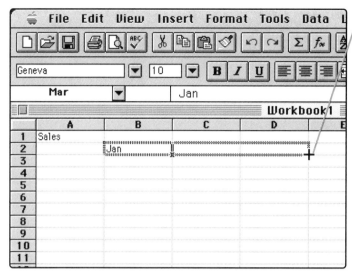

2. **Press and hold** the mouse button as you **drag** the fill handle **across columns C and D**. The border of the cell will expand as you drag.

3. **Release** the button. The AutoFill feature will automatically complete the series for you, as you can see in the next example.

If you want to include six months in the series, simply drag the fill handle across columns E, F, and G. Notice that February and March appeared as abbreviations. If you had typed "January," the succeeding months also would have been spelled out in full.

If you mistakenly fill in more cells in the series than you want, you can erase them. While the cells are highlighted, drag the fill handle backward to erase the unwanted names.

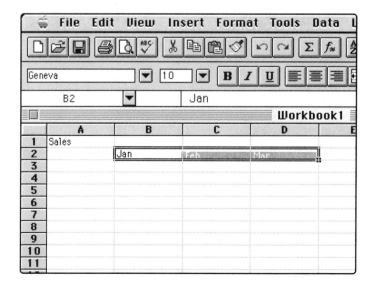

You can also drag the fill handle down the worksheet to create a series in a column format. It's an amazing feature!

# ENTERING ROW HEADINGS

1. **Click** on **A3.** On your screen, the cell will be blank.

2. **Type** the name **Tiler.**

3. **Press Return.** Tiler will be entered into the cell and the border will move to A4.

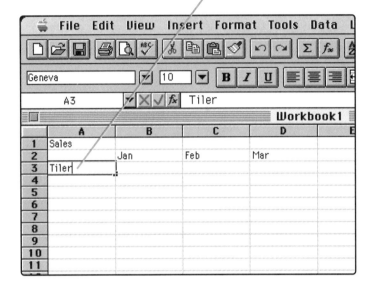

4. **Type** the name **Mackenzie-Smith.**

5. **Press Return.** Notice that the name extends slightly into the next column and covers up the dividing line between columns. It's okay. You'll fix it after all the names are typed.

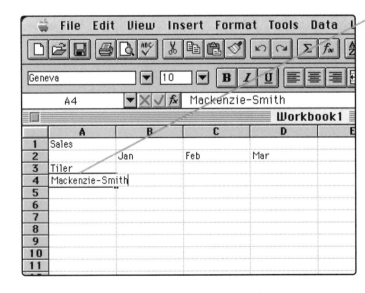

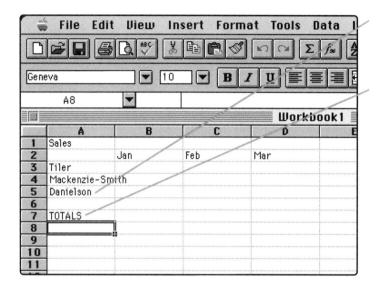

6. **Type** the name **Danielson.**

7. **Press Return twice.**

8. **Type TOTALS** in A7.

9. **Press Return.**

Your worksheet will look like the example to the left.

## CHANGING THE COLUMN WIDTH

In this section, you will change the width of column A to accommodate the long name. You'll love the ease with which this happens.

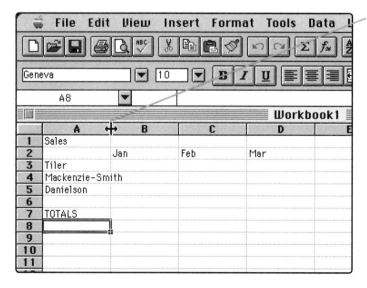

1. **Place** the mouse pointer on the **line between columns A** and **B**. The pointer will change to the shape you see in this example.

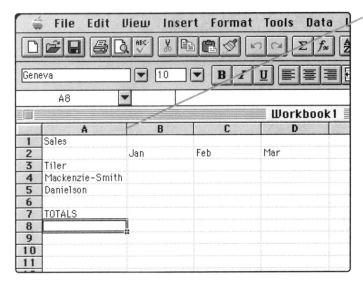

2. **Click twice.** The column will be expanded to a "best fit" width that takes into account the longest entry in the column. (Don't you love it?!) If nothing happens, try a faster speed on the double-clicks.

## SORTING DATA ALPHABETICALLY

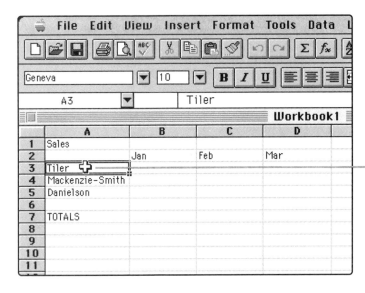

The capability to sort data after it has been entered in the worksheet is a helpful feature of Excel. In this section, you will sort the names in column A alphabetically.

1. **Click** on **A3** and leave the pointer in the middle of the cell. Make sure the pointer looks like a white plus sign.

2. **Press and hold** the mouse button and **drag** the pointer down to **A5.**

Notice that while the mouse button is pressed the cell reference area indicates that you have highlighted three rows in one column (3Rx1C). This is called a *range* because the cells are adjacent to, or next to, each other.

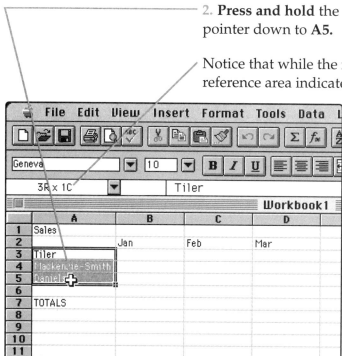

3. **Release** the mouse button when you have highlighted the range A3 through A5.

Notice that the range is highlighted in black except for the first cell, which remains white to tell you that this is the active cell.

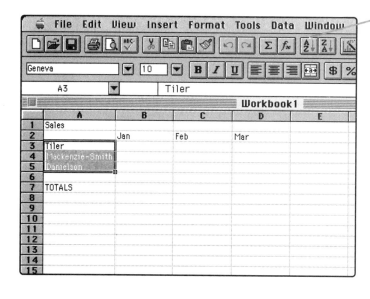

4. **Click** on the **Sort Ascending button** (A to Z) in the toolbar. The names will be sorted alphabetically.

# USING TOOLTIPS

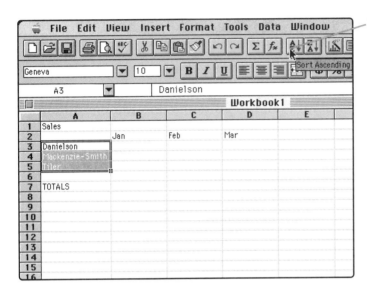

You may have noticed in the previous section that when you placed your pointer on the Sort button, a yellow box describing the button's function appeared. You can use the Tooltips feature for any button at the top of the screen to find out what the button does. Try it!

# ENTERING NUMBERS

**1. Click** on **B3.** On your screen, the cell will be empty.

**2. Type** the number **18453.**

**3. Press** ↓ to enter the number into B3 and automatically move the selection border to B4. Using the arrow keys on your keyboard is another way to enter data and move around the worksheet. (If you are using the arrows on the numeric keypad, make sure that the Num Lock key is turned off.)

**4. Enter** the **numbers** shown on the screen to the left in the appropriate cells on your worksheet.

Remember that there are several ways to confirm that you want to enter data:

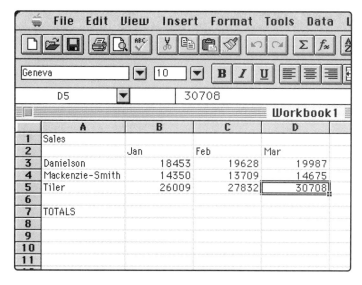

❖ Click on another cell.

❖ Click on ✔.

❖ Press Return. This will enter the data into the cell and move the border to the next cell down.

❖ Press an arrow key on your keyboard to enter the data and move the selection border to the next cell in the direction of the arrow.

❖ Press Enter on the numeric keypad. This will enter the data into the cell and keep you in the selected cell.

Notice that numbers are automatically aligned on the right in a cell. Text is aligned on the left.

This worksheet will be used throughout the rest of this book. In Chapter 2, "Naming and Saving a Workbook," you'll name and save a worksheet. In Chapter 3, "Editing Your Worksheet," you will make corrections to this worksheet.

# Naming and Saving a Workbook

Excel uses standard Macintosh commands to name and save files. In this chapter, you will do the following:

❖ Name a workbook using the Save As command
❖ Save a workbook

## NAMING A WORKBOOK

Use the Save As command to name a workbook.

**1. Press and hold** on **File** in the menu bar. A pull-down menu will appear.

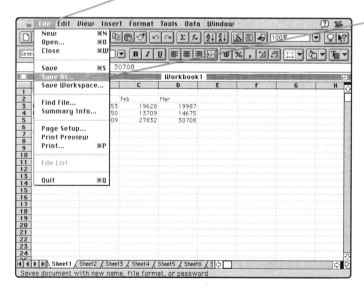

**2. Drag** the highlight bar to **Save As**, then **release** the mouse button. The Save As dialog box will appear. It may appear in a different spot on your screen than you see in the next example.

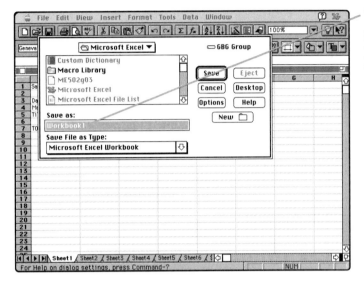

Because Workbook1 in the Save As text box is already highlighted, you can simply begin to type the new filename.

3. **Type Sales Q1**. It will replace the highlighted text.

The top text box indicates that the file will be saved to the Microsoft Excel folder.

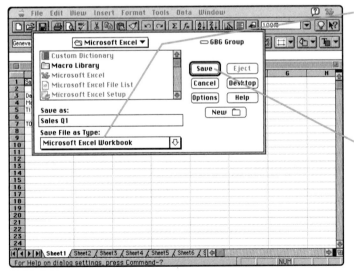

The "Save File as Type" text box indicates that Excel will save this file as an Excel Workbook. If you want to change these designations, see the *User's Guide*.

4. **Click** on **Save**. The Summary Info dialog box will appear.

You don't have to enter anything in the Summary Info dialog box. However, it's useful for future reference to enter information that will help identify a file and its purpose.

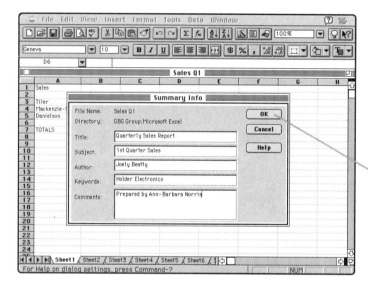

The screen to your left is an example of the kind of information you might want to enter. You can enter data if you want. Press the Tab key to move from one text box to another.

5. **Click** on **OK.** The Summary Info dialog box will close. Your file is then saved.

## SAVING A FILE

Develop the habit of saving your file while you work on it. Save often. This habit will spare you much grief and aggravation in the event of a power failure or equipment problem.

With the Save File button, you can save with a click of your mouse.

1. **Click** on the **Save File button** in the toolbar. A wristwatch will appear briefly as Excel saves your workbook. Do this step often.

# Editing Your Worksheet

Editing is straightforward in Excel because of one of Excel's newest features, in-cell editing, which allows you to edit the contents of a cell directly in the cell. Using the mouse gives you a great deal of control in the editing process. You can change the contents of a cell, change individual letters or numbers in a cell, clear a cell completely, or even undo your edit if you change your mind. In this chapter, you will do the following:

❖ Make edits to the worksheet you created in Chapter 1 so that you can use the worksheet throughout the rest of this book
❖ Cancel an edit
❖ Use Undo

## ADDING DATA

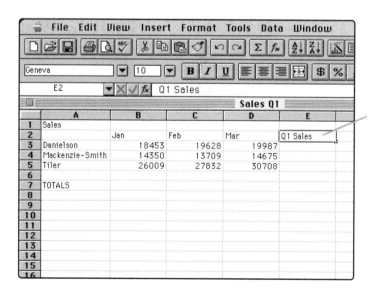

You can add data at any time to a worksheet. In this section, you will add the heading "Q1 Sales" to Column E.

1. **Click** on **E2**. On your screen, it will be blank.

2. **Type Q1 Sales** and press **Return**.

# INSERTING A CHARACTER INTO A CELL

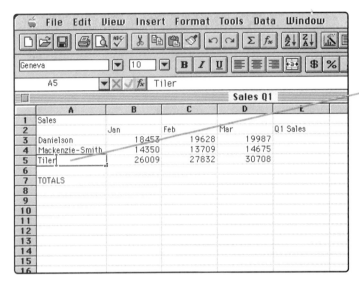

In this section, you will change the name "Tiler" to "Tiller" with in-cell editing.

1. **Click twice** on Tiler in **A5**. Your cursor will begin flashing in the cell, Tiler will appear in the contents box, and the pointer will become an I-beam.

2. **Place the I-beam** between the letters *l* and *e* and **click** to place the flashing cursor.

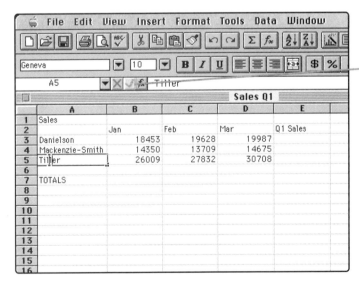

3. **Type** the letter **l.** It will be added to the name.

4. **Click** on ✔ or press **Return** to enter the change in the cell.

# DELETING A CHARACTER FROM A CELL

In this section, you will change the name "Mackenzie-Smith" to "McKenzie-Smith."

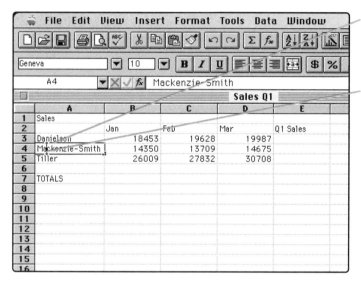

1. **Click twice** on Mackenzie-Smith in **A4**. The pointer will change to an I-beam.

2. **Place** the **I-beam** between the letters *a* and *c*.

3. **Click** to set the flashing cursor in place.

4. **Press** the **Delete key** to delete the letter *a*.

# REPLACING A CHARACTER

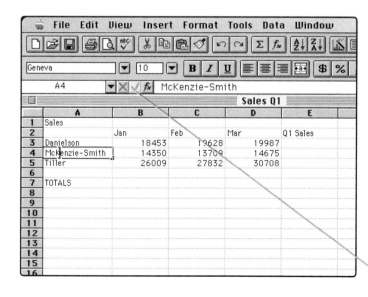

1. **Place** the **I-beam** between the letters *c* and *k*. Click to place the flashing cursor.

2. **Press and hold** the mouse button as you drag the highlight bar over the "k," then release the mouse buttton.

3. **Type** a capital **K** to make the name McKenzie.

4. **Click** on ✔.

# DELETING MORE THAN ONE CHARACTER

You can edit the contents of a cell in the contents box. In this section, you will change the name "Danielson" to "Daniels."

1. **Click** *once* on Danielson in **A3.**

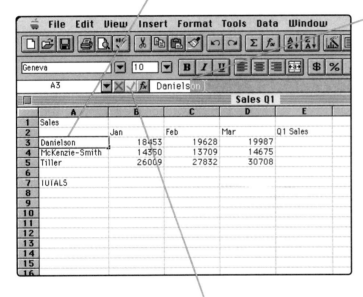

2. **Move** the mouse pointer up to the contents box and **place** it at the **end** of the **word**. The pointer will change to an I-beam.

3. **Press and hold** the **mouse button** as you **drag** the highlight bar over the **last two letters** in the name.

4. **Release** the mouse button.

5. **Press** the **Delete** key to delete the letters.

6. **Click** on ✔ or **press Return** to confirm the change.

# CANCELING AN EDIT

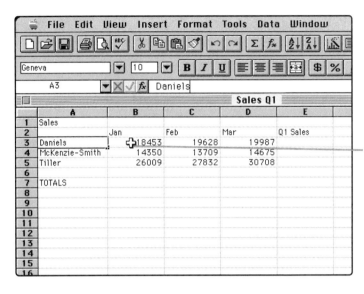

If you're like the rest of us, you occasionally make a change you didn't intend to make. If you catch the mistake before you confirm the change, you can undo it.

1. **Place** the plus-sign **pointer** to the **left** of the number in **B3**.

2. **Click twice**. The cursor will change into an I-beam.

3. **Click twice again**. The contents of the cell will be highlighted.

4. **Type** the number **2000.** It will replace the highlighted number. (Do *not* press Return!)

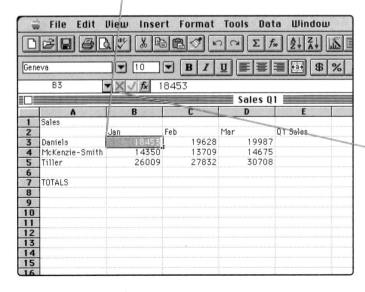

At this point, you discover that you should not have changed the number. Because you are still in the cell and have not pressed Return, you can simply cancel the change.

5. **Click** on the ✕ (the Cancel button) in the edit bar to undo the change. The original number, 18453, will appear again.

# USING UNDO

If you actually enter a change and then decide that you don't want it, you can undo the change with the Undo button as long as you use it before you perform any other function.

In this section, you will clear the contents of a cell and then undo the change.

1. **Click** once on TOTALS in **A7**.

2. **Press** the **Delete key**. The contents of the cell will be cleared.

3. **Click** on **B7**.

4. **Click** on the **Undo button** in the toolbar. The contents of A7 will be restored and the selection border will move back to A7. Even though you moved to a new cell, you did not perform an actual function, such as entering data or using a menu bar command. Therefore, you can use the Undo button.

A general rule of thumb is that you can use the ✕ (Cancel button) when it is visible. If it is not visible, use the Undo button.

# Totaling Columns and Rows

This is the fun part! Excel 5 has a wonderful icon that contains a built-in formula to sum columns and rows. You can total individual columns and rows and then use features such as AutoFill and Fill Right to copy the formula to other columns and rows. Or, you can highlight a range of cells and use the AutoSum button to total all columns and rows with one command. In this chapter, you will do the following:

❖ Use the AutoSum button to sum columns and rows

## USING THE AUTOSUM BUTTON

Although you can write a formula to total a column or row, clicking on the AutoSum button creates the formula for you automatically. (You will learn how to write formulas in Chapter 13, "Writing Formulas and Using the Subtotal Feature.")

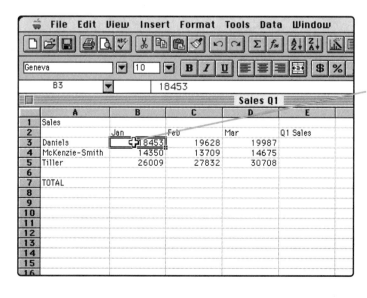

## Highlighting a Range

1. **Click** on **B3**. Leave the pointer in the cell.

2. **Press and hold** the mouse button and **drag** the pointer down to **E7**. The range B3 to E7 will be highlighted.

3. **Click** on the **AutoSum button** in the toolbar. ($\Sigma$ is the Greek symbol for *sum*.) Sums will appear in column E and row 7.

4. **Click anywhere** in the worksheet to remove the highlighting.

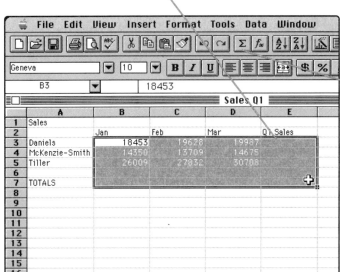

Your screen will look like this example.

5. **Click** on the **Save button** in the toolbar to save your work.

# Using Page Setup, Print Preview, and Printing a File

When you print a file in Excel, you can customize the printed page in a number of ways. For example, you can add identifying information to a file with headers and footers. You can remove the gridlines you see on your screen and center the worksheet horizontally and vertically on the page. You can even preview a file to see what it will look like before it prints. In this chapter, you will do the following:

❖ Print a worksheet
❖ Use the Page Setup options
❖ Add a header to a file
❖ Use the Print Preview feature

## USING THE PRINT BUTTON

1. **Click** on the **Print button** in the toolbar. A Printing message box will appear.

| | File | Edit | View | Insert | Format | Tools | Data | Window |
|---|---|---|---|---|---|---|---|---|

| Geneva | | 10 | | **B** | *I* | U | | | | | $ | % |

| A1 | | | Sales |

**Sales Q1**

| | A | B | C | D | E |
|---|---|---|---|---|---|
| 1 | Sales | | | | |
| 2 | | Jan | Feb | Mar | Q1 Sales |
| 3 | Daniels | 18453 | 19628 | 19987 | 58068 |
| 4 | McKenzie-Smith | 14350 | 13709 | 14675 | 42734 |
| 5 | Tiller | 26009 | 27832 | 30708 | 84549 |
| 6 | | | | | |
| 7 | TOTALS | 58812 | 61169 | 65370 | 185351 |
| 8 | | | | | |
| 9 | | | | | |
| 10 | | | | | |
| 11 | | | | | |
| 12 | | | | | |
| 13 | | | | | |
| 14 | | | | | |
| 15 | | | | | |
| 16 | | | | | |

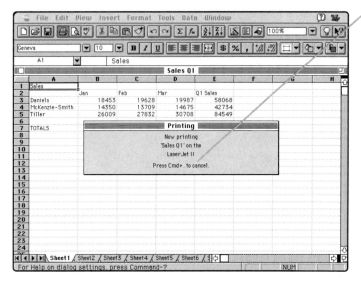

Notice that you can press and hold the Command key while you press the . (period) key if you want to cancel the print command. Because the file is short, the message box will appear only briefly. It will be on the screen for a longer time for a longer file.

## USING PAGE SETUP OPTIONS

You can customize many features of printing in Excel by using Page Setup options. The settings you make in the Page Setup dialog box affect only this particular worksheet. If you have multiple worksheets in a file (as you will in Part III), you have to do Page Setup options for each worksheet.

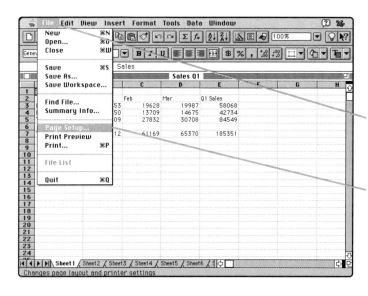

## Opening the Page Setup Dialog Box

1. **Press and hold** on **File** in the menu bar. A pull-down menu will appear.

2. **Drag** the highlight bar to **Page Setup**, then release the mouse button. The Page Setup dialog box will appear.

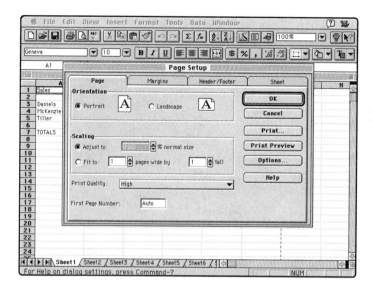

The Page Setup dialog box has four sections, or tabs: Page, Margins, Header/Footer, and Sheet. First you will go to the Margins section.

## Centering the Worksheet on the Printed Page

You can center your worksheet both horizontally and vertically on the printed page. This will have no effect on how the worksheet appears on the screen. In this example, you will center the worksheet horizontally.

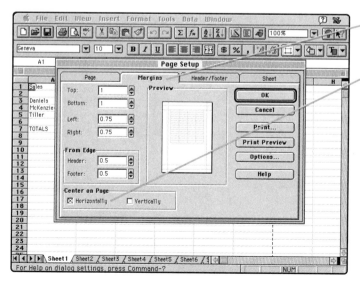

1. **Click** on the **Margins Tab** to go to the Margins options.

2. **Click** on **Horizontally** to insert an X in the box. When the file prints, the worksheet will be centered across the page.

# Changing Margins

The worksheet is set up with standard (default) margins of 1 inch at the top and bottom and .75 inch on the left and right. In this example, you will change the top margin to 2 inches.

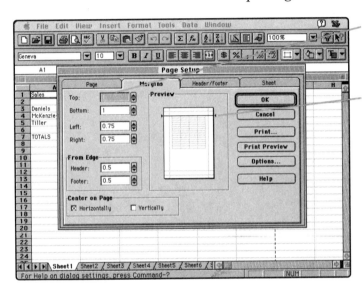

1. **Click twice** in the **Top Margin box.** The box will be highlighted.

Notice that a bold line appears in the Preview box in the top margin position, indicating that the top margin is currently selected.

2. **Type 2**. It will replace the highlighted text.

# Adding a Header

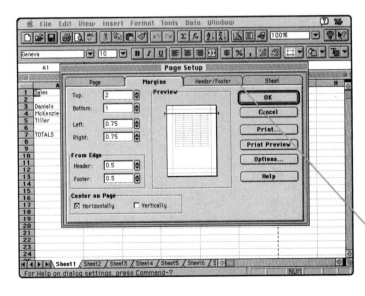

A *header* is a line of type added to the top of the printed page. It usually contains identifying data, such as the filename or the date, but it can be any text you want. A header can be aligned with the left margin, centered, or aligned with the right margin.

1. **Click** on the **Header/ Footer Tab** to move to the Header/Footer options.

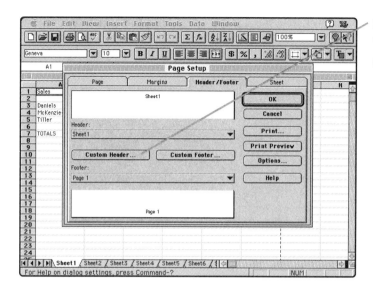

**2. Click** on **Custom Header**. The Header dialog box will appear.

**3. Click** in the **Center Section box** to place the cursor.

**4. Press and hold** the mouse button and **drag** the highlight bar over the &[Tab], then release the mouse button. (This code prints the name you give to Sheet1 in the header. You'll learn how to name Sheet1 in the section entitled "Naming Worksheets," in Chapter 11.)

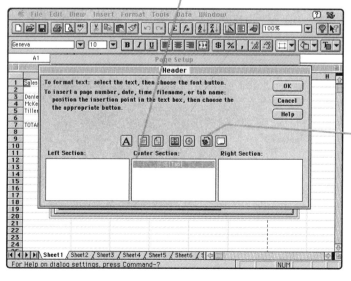

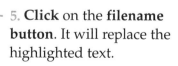

**5. Click** on the **filename button**. It will replace the highlighted text.

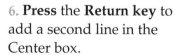

**6. Press** the **Return key** to add a second line in the Center box.

7. **Click** on the **date button**. The code for date will be inserted in the box.

The other icons in this dialog box insert the following information:

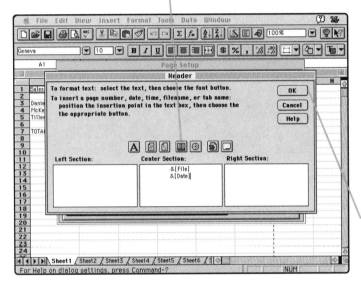

 Brings up the font dialog box

 Page number

 Number of pages in a document

 Time of printing

 Sheet name

8. **Click** on **OK**. The Header/Footer options will reappear.

# Deleting a Footer

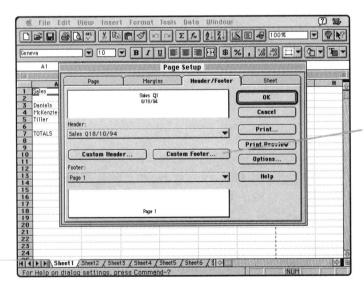

Your worksheet is set up to print "Page 1" at the bottom of the page. In this example, you will delete the page number.

1. **Click** on the **Custom Footer button**. The Footer dialog box will appear.

2. **Click** to the **left** of **Page &[Page]** in the center box. This code prints the word "Page" and then the page number.

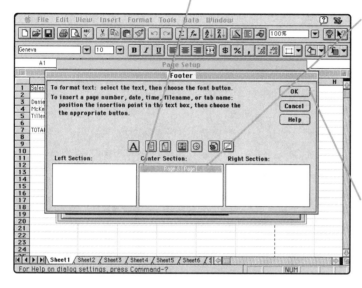

3. **Press and hold** the mouse button and **drag** the cursor across **Page &[Page]** in the Center Section box. The text will be highlighted.

4. **Press** the **Delete key** on your keyboard. The text will be deleted.

5. **Click** on **OK**. The Header/Footer options will reappear.

# Removing Gridlines From the Printed Page

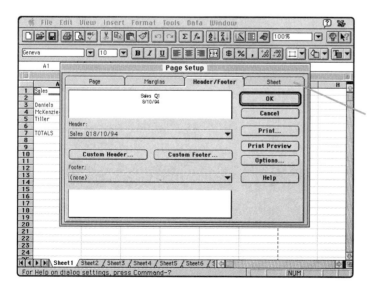

Your page will print with the same gridlines you see on your screen unless you remove them.

1. **Click** on the **Sheet Tab**. The Sheet options will appear.

2. **Click** on **Gridlines** to *remove* the × from the box. If you leave the × in the box, the worksheet will print with gridlines on it. Removing the gridlines from the printed page will not affect the gridlines on your screen.

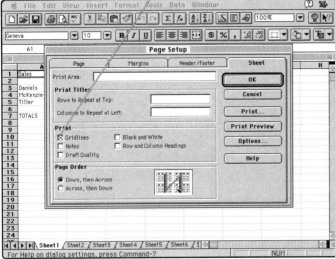

## Increasing the Size of the Worksheet on the Printed Page

You can significantly enlarge the size of the worksheet on the printed page. This capacity is especially helpful if you plan to use the page in a presentation.

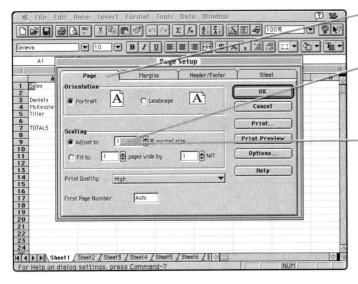

1. **Click** on the **Page Tab**. The Page options will appear.

2. **Click** to the **right** of "**100**" in the Adjust to box to set the cursor.

3. **Press and hold** the mouse button and **drag** the cursor backward **over** the **00** in 100. The 0s will be highlighted.

4. **Release** the mouse button.

5. **Type 25** to make the enlargement factor 125%. Experiment with different sizes. If you want a smaller print size than normal, type a number less than 100. (This size affects the printout only. To change the size of the type on your printout *and* on the screen, see the section, "Increasing Type Size," in Chapter 9.

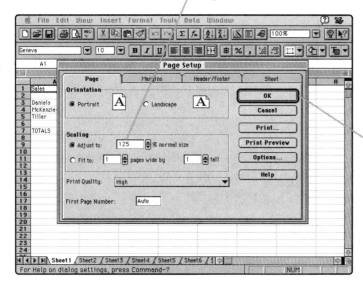

6. **Click** on **OK**. The Sales Q1 worksheet will appear.

## PREVIEWING THE PAGE

1. **Click** on the **Print Preview button** in the toolbar. The Print Preview dialog box will appear.

# Using the Zoom Feature

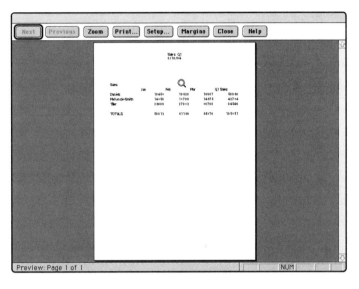

In the Preview screen, the pointer looks like a magnifying glass.

1. **Place** the **magnifying glass** over the worksheet **area** you want to see more closely.

2. **Click** the **mouse button**. The area you selected will be enlarged.

3. **Click** the **mouse button** again to return to the full-page view.

# Changing the Margins Through the Preview Screen

Notice that the header appears at the top of the page and is not affected by the position of the top margin.

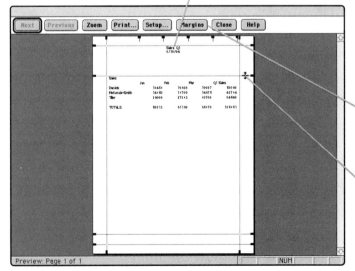

In the Print Preview screen, you can change margins with your mouse. In this section, you will change the top margin back to 1 inch.

1. **Click** on the **Margins button** if the margin lines are not showing.

2. **Place** the mouse pointer on the **handle** (the black square) on the **top margin line**. The pointer will change to the shape you see in this example.

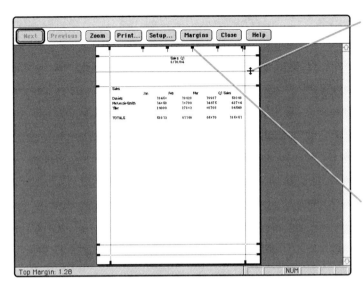

3. **Press and hold** the **mouse button** as you **drag** the line up so that it is approximately 1 inch from the top of the page.

4. **Release** the mouse button when the line is positioned where you want it.

You can change the column width by dragging the column handles using the same method.

# PRINTING THROUGH THE PRINT PREVIEW SCREEN

1. **Click** on **Print** to print the document. The Print dialog box will appear. (**Or click** on **Close** to close the Preview screen without printing.)

Your Print dialog box may look different, depending on your printer.

**2. Click** on **Selected Sheet(s)** to put a dot in the circle if one is not already there. This step will print only the worksheet on which you are currently working.

**3. Click** on **Print**. A Printing message box will appear and your worksheet will print.

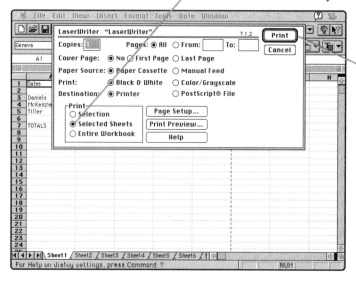

You can also print by using the menu bar.

**1. Press and hold** on **File** in the menu bar. A pull-down menu will appear.

**2. Drag** the highlight bar to **Print**, then **release** the mouse button. The Print dialog box shown above will appear.

# Closing A Workbook and Exiting Excel

In Macintosh-based programs, you can often accomplish the same task several different ways. Excel 5 is no exception. In this chapter you will do the following:

❖ Learn a quick way to close a workbook
❖ Learn a quick way to exit Excel

## CLOSING A WORKBOOK

When you close a workbook, you do not exit Excel. If no other workbooks are open, the empty Excel Window will appear.

1. **Click** on the **Close box** (☐) on the left side of the title bar. A Microsoft Excel dialog box will appear.

2. **Click** on **Yes**.

If you click on No, any changes you made to the file since the last time you saved will be lost. If you click on Cancel, the dialog box will disappear and you will be returned to the worksheet.

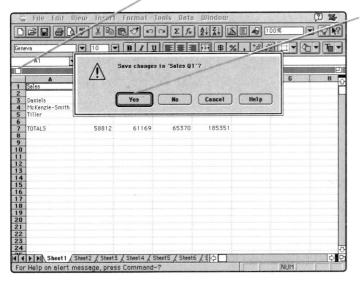

## EXITING EXCEL

If you have been following along with the steps in this chapter, you closed the Sales Q1 workbook and the empty Excel window is on your screen. If you did not close the workbook on your screen, this exit procedure will work anyway.

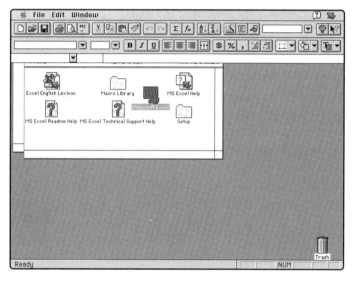

1. **Press ⌘-Q**. If you saved before doing this, Excel will close.

If you forgot to save, Excel will rescue you and ask whether you want to save.

2. **Click** on **Yes** to save and exit Excel.

## OPENING EXCEL

If you want to continue to Chapter 7, "Opening a Saved Workbook," reopen Excel.

1. **Click twice** on the **Microsoft Excel icon**. The Excel opening screen will appear.

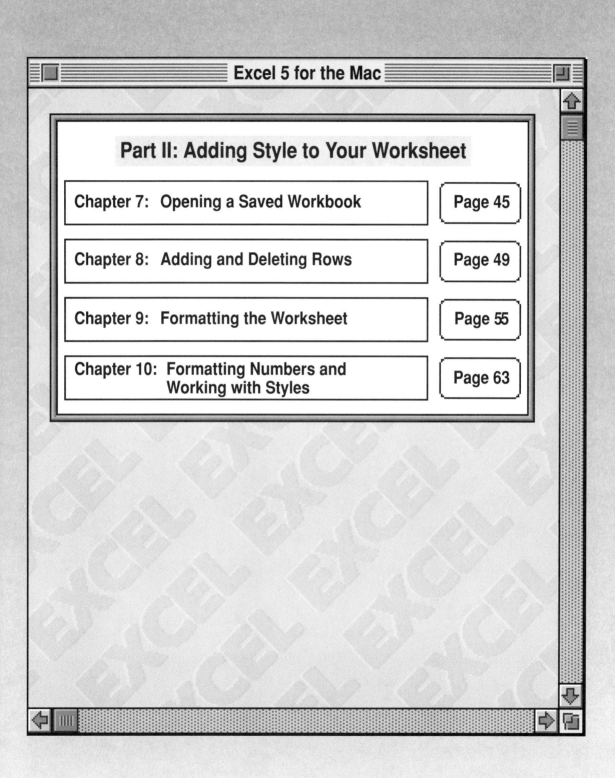

**Excel 5 for the Mac**

# Part II: Adding Style to Your Worksheet

# Opening a Saved Workbook

Excel makes opening a saved workbook file as easy as clicking your mouse. In this chapter, you will do the following:

❖ Open the Sales Q1 file by using the File pull-down menu
❖ Open the Sales Q1 file by using the Open File button

## OPENING A SAVED WORKBOOK

Excel has a special feature in the file pull-down menu that makes opening a saved workbook file especially easy.

## Method #1

1. **Press and hold** on **File** in the menu bar. A pull-down menu will appear.

The File pull-down menu lists the four most recent files that were opened. If others have used Excel before you, there may be up to four filenames on the list. As you create workbooks, the list will change.

2. **Drag** the **highlight bar** to **Sales Q1**, then release the mouse button. The workbook will appear.

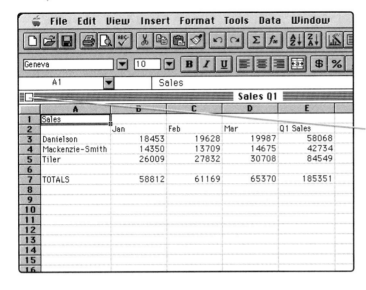

If you want to try method #2, you need to close Sales Q1 first. Because you have made no changes to Sales Q1, there is no need to save.

3. **Click** on the **Close box** (☐) on the left side of the title bar. A "save changes" dialog box will appear.

4. **Click** on **No**.

## Method #2

Excel has a button on the toolbar for locating and opening a workbook file.

1. **Click** on the **Open File button** on the toolbar. The Open dialog box will appear.

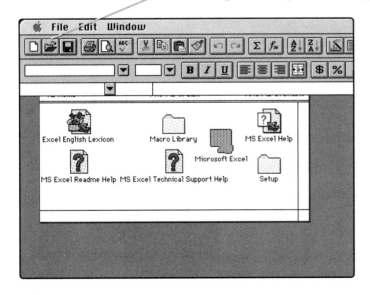

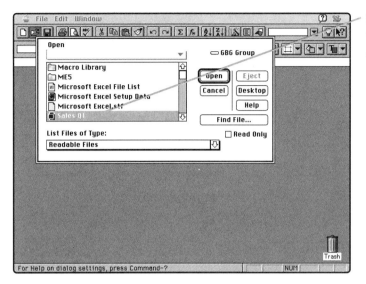

2. **Click twice** on **Sales Q1**. The Sales Q1 workbook will open.

# Adding and Deleting Rows

As part of the process of adding and deleting rows, you will use an Excel feature called a shortcut menu. If you think that clicking on the menu bar and getting a pull-down menu is easy, just wait until you use a shortcut menu! In this chapter, you will do the following;

❖ Add rows
❖ Delete a row
❖ Use a shortcut menu

## ADDING ROWS

Suppose that you want the company name on the Sales Q1 worksheet for a presentation tomorrow. In this section, you will add three rows at the beginning of the Sales Q1 worksheet so that you can add the company name. You will also add some other blank rows within the worksheet.

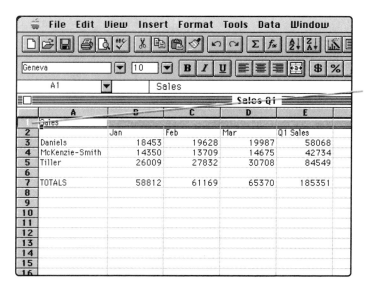

## Using a Shortcut Menu

1. **Click** on the **row 1 button**. The entire row will be highlighted. Leave the mouse pointer on the row.

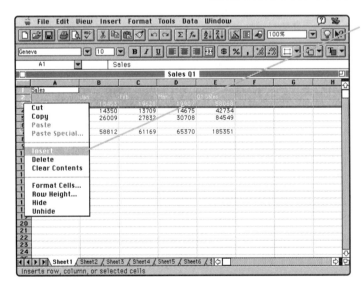

2. **Press and hold** the mouse button and **drag** the highlight bar down to **row 3**, then **release** the mouse button. *Leave the mouse pointer in the highlighted area.* When you are getting ready to use a shortcut menu, it's important that you leave the mouse pointer in the highlighted area or the next step won't work.

3. **Press and hold** the **Control key** as you **press and hold** the **mouse button**. A shortcut menu will appear.

4. **Release** the **Control key** and **drag** the highlight bar to **Insert**, then **release** the mouse button. Three rows will be inserted at the top of the worksheet. All following rows will be renumbered. Excel knew to insert rows because you used the row buttons to select the number of rows to be added.

5. **Click** on the **row 5 button**. The entire row will be highlighted. Leave the pointer in the cell.

6. **Press and hold** the **Control key** as you **press and hold** the **mouse button**. A shortcut menu will appear.

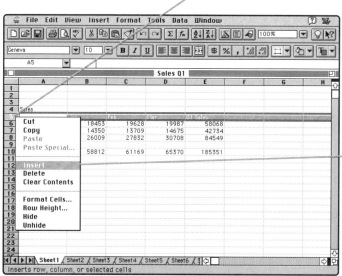

7. **Release** the **Control key** and **drag** the highlight bar to **Insert**, then **release** the mouse button. A row will be inserted at the cursor point. All following rows will be renumbered.

## Using the Insert Menu

In this example, you will add a row above the names by using the Insert pull-down menu.

1. **Click** on Daniels in **A7**.

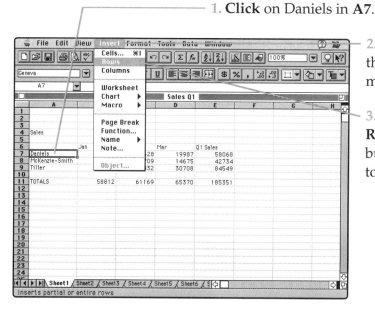

2. **Press and hold** on **Insert** in the menu bar. A pull-down menu will appear.

3. **Drag** the highlight bar to **Rows**, then **release** the mouse button. A row will be added to the worksheet.

# DELETING A ROW

After looking at your worksheet, you decide that three rows at the top are too many. Don't worry. Deleting is easy.

1. **Click** on the **row 1 button**. This step will select the entire row. Leave the pointer in the row.

2. **Press** the **Control key** as you **press and hold** the mouse button. A shortcut menu will appear.

3. **Drag** the highlight bar to **Delete**, then **release** the mouse button. The highlighted row will be deleted and all following rows will be renumbered.

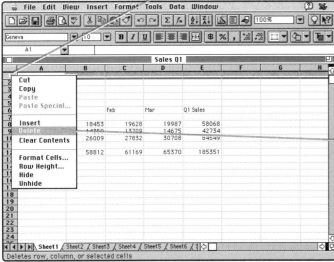

Your worksheet will look like this example.

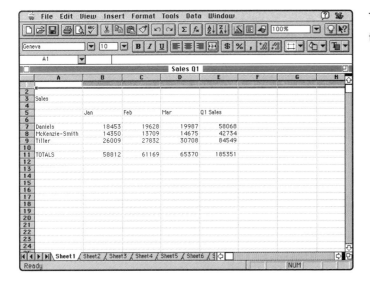

# ADDING A WORKSHEET HEADING

In this section, you will add the company name to the worksheet and change "Sales" to a more descriptive heading.

1. **Click** on **A1**. On your screen, the cell will be empty.

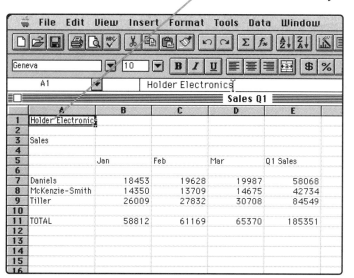

2. **Type Holder Electronics**. Don't be concerned that the name is too long for the cell. As long as the cell to the right is empty, the entry will expand into the next cell.

3. **Press Return** to insert the name into A1. You will center the company name over the worksheet in the section "Centering Across Columns and Within Cells," in Chapter 9.

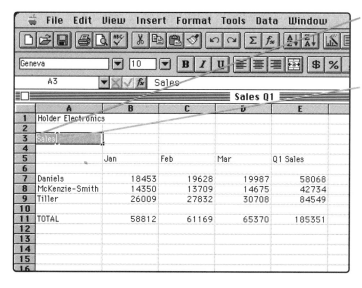

4. **Click twice** on Sales in **A3** to activate the cell for in-cell editing.

5. With the I-beam in the cell, **click twice**. The contents of the cell will be highlighted.

6. **Type** the words **Quarterly Sales Report**. They will replace the highlighted text.

7. **Press Return** to insert "Quarterly Sales Report" in A3.

8. **Click** on the **Save button** on the toolbar to save the changes in your worksheet.

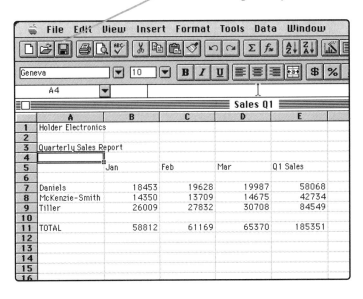

In the next chapter, you will dress up the worksheet with larger type, boldface print, and other style changes.

# Formatting the Worksheet

Excel has many buttons available right on the toolbar that will help improve the appearance of your worksheet. These buttons make formatting your worksheet a snap. In this chapter, you will do the following:

❖ Increase the font size
❖ Change the type style to bold
❖ Change the type style to italic
❖ Underline text
❖ Add a border to a cell
❖ Center across columns and within cells

## INCREASING FONT SIZE

Notice that Excel is set up to print with a Geneva font, or type style, in a 10-point size. In this section, you will learn how to increase font size.

1. **Click** on Holder Electronics in **A1**.

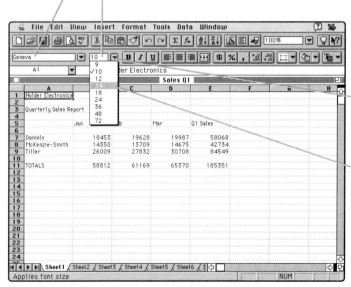

Notice that the toolbar shows Geneva as the font and the size as 10 points.

2. **Press and hold** on the ▼ next to the font size. A pull-down list will appear.

3. **Drag** the highlight bar to **14**, then **release** the mouse button to increase the font size of the selected text to 14 points. Holder Electronics will change to 14 points on your screen.

4. **Click** on Quarterly Sales Report in **A3**.

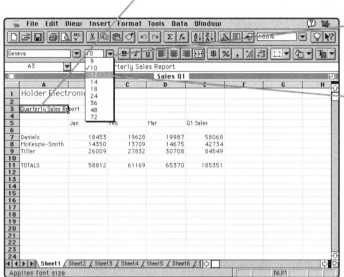

5. **Press and hold** the ▼ next to the font size. A pull-down list will appear.

6. **Drag** the highlight bar to **12**, then **release** the mouse button to increase the font size of the selected text to 12 points. "Quarterly Sales Report" will change to 12-point size on your screen.

## A Note About Appearances

Even though "Quarterly Sales Report" appears to extend into cell B3, Excel considers it to be in cell A3. Therefore, when you click on A3, all three words

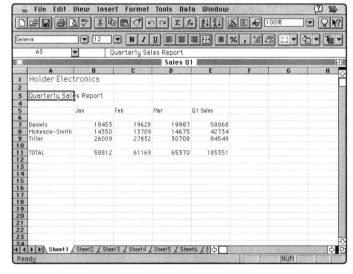

show in the edit line. Try clicking on cell B3. Notice that nothing shows in the edit line because nothing was actually entered into cell B3. Interesting. . . .

Notice also when you click on B3 that the font size shown in the Font Size box is 10. The reason is that you applied the 12-point size to A3, not to B3.

# ADDING AND REMOVING BOLD FROM TYPE

In Excel, many buttons work like toggle switches. Click to turn the function on and then click again to turn it off. In this section, you will make text bold, then turn off the bold, and then turn it on again. First, select the cell you want to change.

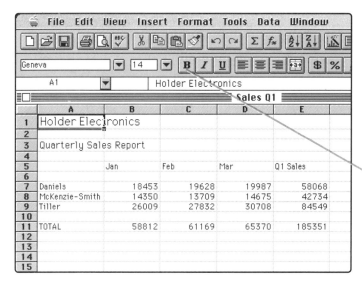

**1. Click** on Holder Electronics in **A1**.

**2. Click** on the **Bold button** on the toolbar (the large B). The text in A1 will be made bold.

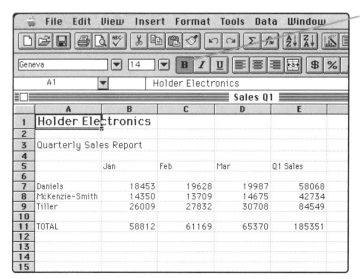

Notice that the Bold button now appears darker and pressed in. This tells you that this feature is currently turned on for the cell.

3. While the cell is still selected, **click** on the **Bold button** again to make the type normal.

4. **Click** on the **Bold button** again to make the text bold once more.

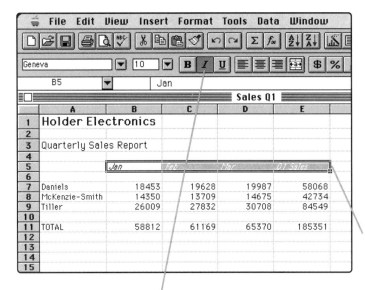

# MAKING TEXT ITALIC

In this section, you will highlight a range of cells and, with one command, apply italics to the entire range.

1. **Click** on Jan in **B5**. Leave the pointer in the cell.

2. **Press and hold** the mouse button and **drag** the pointer over to Q1 Sales in **E5**. Then release the mouse button.

3. **Click** on the **Italics button** on the toolbar (the large, slanted I). The text in all the cells will be italicized.

# UNDERLINING TEXT

If you have been following along with these examples, cells B5 through E5 are highlighted.

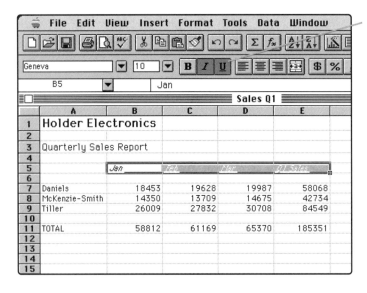

1. **Click** on the **Underline button** on the toolbar (the large, underlined U). The highlighted text from the previous section will be underlined.

2. **Click anywhere** on the worksheet to remove the highlighting so that you can see the italics and underlining in cells B5 through E5.

# CREATING A DOUBLE UNDERLINE

In this section, you will put a double underline beneath the totals in row 11.

1. **Click** on **B11**. Leave the pointer in the cell.

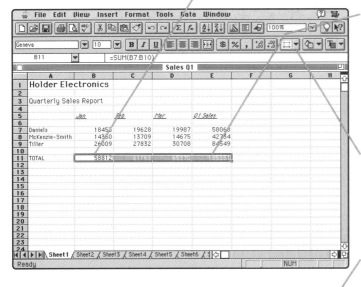

2. **Press and hold** the mouse button and **drag** the pointer over to **E11**.

3. **Release** the mouse button when you have highlighted B11 through E11.

4. **Press and hold** the ▼ to the right of the Borders button in the toolbar. The Borders box will appear.

5. **Drag** the pointer to the **double underline button**, then **release** the mouse button. The Borders box will disappear and B11 through E11 will be underlined.

6. **Click anywhere** on the worksheet to remove the highlighting so that you can see the double underline.

Notice that the double underline border is applied to the cell itself. This contrasts with the underline feature in the previous section, which was applied to the *contents* of the cell.

# CENTERING ACROSS COLUMNS

Text in a cell is normally aligned on the left. In this section, you will highlight rows 1 through 3 and apply the centering option to all of them at the same time.

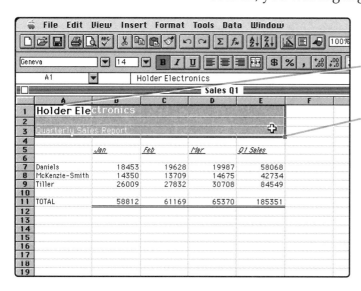

1. **Click** on **A1**. Leave the pointer in the cell.

2. **Press and hold** the mouse button and **drag** the pointer diagonally down to **E3**.

3. **Release** the mouse button when you have highlighted cells A1 through E3.

4. **Click** on the **Center Across Columns button** on the toolbar. The company name and worksheet title will be centered across the highlighted columns.

5. **Click anywhere** on the worksheet to remove the highlighting and see the centering.

# CENTERING WITHIN CELLS

In this example, you will center the text in row 5 in each cell.

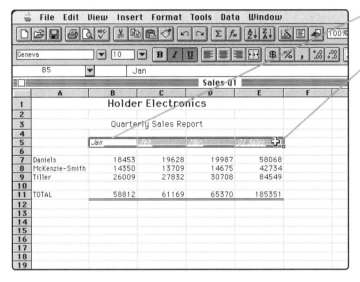

1. **Click** on **B5**. Leave the pointer in the cell.

2. **Press and hold** the mouse button and **drag** the pointer horizontally across to **E5**.

3. **Release** the mouse button when you have highlighted cells B1 through E5.

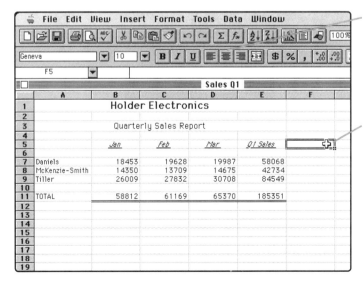

4. **Click** on the **Center button** on the toolbar. The column headers in the table will be centered in their respective cells.

5. **Click anywhere** on the worksheet to remove the highlighting and see the centering.

You will format the numbers on the worksheet in the next chapter.

# Formatting Numbers and Working with Styles

The standard (or default) style for numbers is called the Normal number style. You can change this style and format numbers so that they appear with dollar signs, commas, decimals, or percentages. Numbers can be rounded off to a specific decimal place or whole number or made to appear with a minus sign or parentheses to indicate a negative number. You can format numbers to appear as dates or times, or in the specialized style called scientific notation. You can even save specific formatting as a style and then apply that style to another set of numbers. In this chapter, you will do the following:

❖ Format the numbers already in a worksheet
❖ Format non-adjacent cells with a single command
❖ Save a specific format as a style and apply that style to other numbers
❖ Remove and restore styles in a worksheet

## INSERTING COMMAS IN NUMBERS

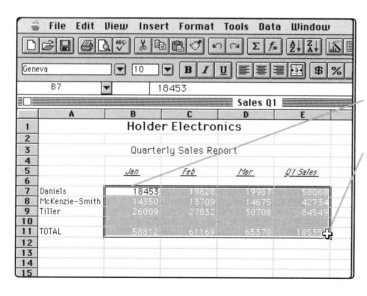

In this example, you will apply the comma style to the numbers on the worksheet.

1. **Click** on **B7**. Leave the pointer in the cell.

2. **Press and hold** the mouse button and **drag** the pointer diagonally down to **E11**. Then release the mouse button.

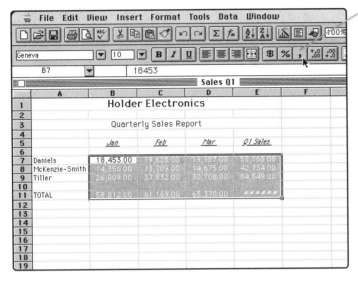

3. **Click** on the **Comma button** on the toolbar.

Notice that some of the numbers have changed to number signs (#). Don't panic. This simply means that the numbers are now too long for the cells because the comma style includes two decimal places. If you want the decimal places to show, you can change the cell width, as you did in the section entitled "Changing the Column Width," in Chapter 1. In this example, you will remove the decimal places.

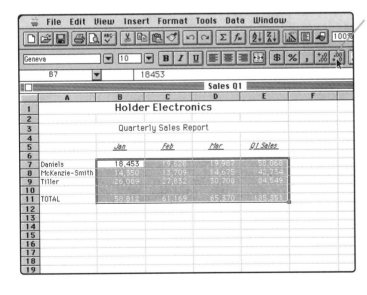

4. **Click twice** on the **Decrease Decimal button** on the toolbar. Each click will remove a zero.

# ADDING DOLLAR SIGNS

In this section, you will use the Format menu rather than a toolbar button to add the Currency style to the first and last rows of numbers. If you use the Command (⌘) key, you can highlight non-adjacent rows (or columns or cells) and apply a command to all highlighted areas at one time.

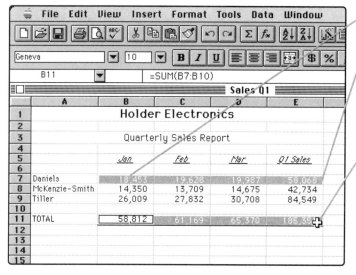

1. **Click** on **B7**. Leave the pointer in the cell.

2. **Press and hold** the mouse button and **drag** the pointer over to **E7**. Then **release** the mouse button.

3. **Press and hold** the ⌘ **key** and **repeat steps 1 and 2** to highlight cells B11:E11. (B11:E11 is another way to say B11 through E11.) Make sure to leave the mouse pointer in the highlighted area or the next step won't work.

4. **Press and hold** the **Control key** as you **press** the mouse button. A shortcut menu will appear.

5. **Drag** the highlight bar to **Format Cells**, then **release** the mouse button. The Format Cells dialog box will appear.

6. **Click** on **Currency** in the Category list.

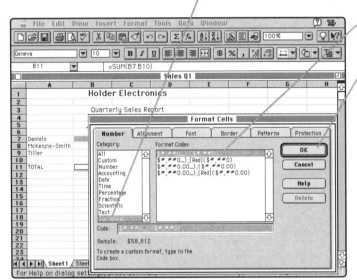

7. **Click** on **$#,##0_);($#,##0)** in the Format Codes list.

8. **Click** on **OK**.

Depending on the version of the Geneva font you have, the number in E11 may still be too long for the cell. If so, use the mouse to increase the width of column E. Refer to "Changing the Column Width," in Chapter 1, if you need help.

## NAMING A STYLE

Number format, font, borders, and alignment are some of the elements that make up the *style* of a cell. If you use a certain style frequently, you can save it as a Named Style and then apply the Named Style to

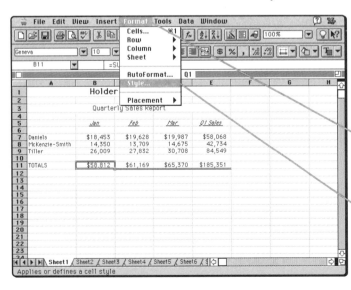

another cell or range. In this section, you will select cell B11 and name the style of the cell "totals."

1. **Click** on **B11**.

2. **Press and hold** on **Format** in the menu bar. A pull-down menu will appear.

3. **Drag** the highlight bar to **Style**, then **release** the mouse button. The Style dialog box will appear.

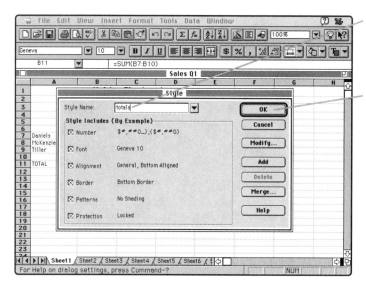

4. **Type totals**. It will replace the highlighted text in the Style Name box.

5. **Click** on **OK**. The formatting in B11 is now saved as the style "totals."

## REMOVING AND RESTORING FORMATS AND STYLES

If you decide that you don't like a particular format or style, you can remove it with the Undo command if you use it immediately after applying the style. There are, however, other ways to remove unwanted styles.

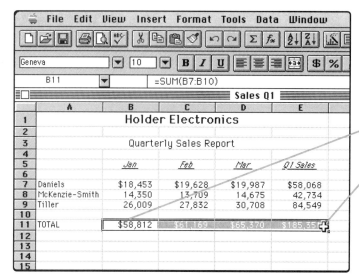

## Clearing Formats

1. **Click** on **B11** and leave the pointer in the cell.

2. **Press and hold** the mouse button and **drag** the highlight bar across to **E11**.

3. **Press and hold** on **Edit** in the menu bar. A pull-down menu will appear.

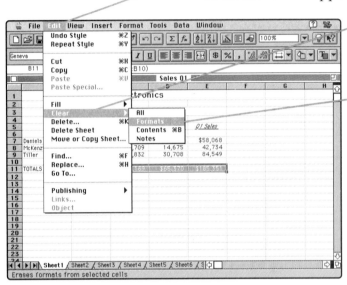

4. **Drag** the highlight bar to **Clear**. A second menu will appear.

5. **Drag** the highlight bar to **Formats**, then **release** the mouse button. The worksheet will reappear. The formatting styles you applied to the highlighted cells will be removed.

# Applying a Named Style

First highlight the cell or range to which you want to apply a Named Style. If you have been following along with these examples, B11:E11 is already highlighted.

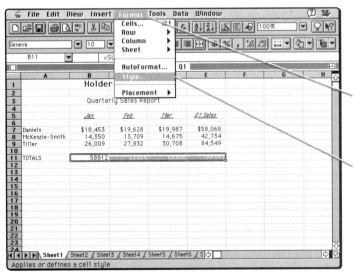

1. **Press and hold** on **Format** in the menu bar. A pull-down menu will appear.

2. **Drag** the highlight bar to **Style**, then **release** the mouse button. The Style dialog box will appear.

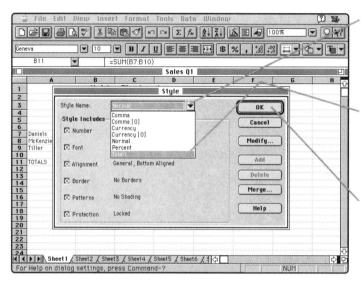

3. **Press and hold** on the ▼ to the right of the Style Name box. A drop-down list will appear.

4. **Drag** the mouse pointer to "**total**." The drop-down list will disappear and "totals" will be in the Style Name box.

5. **Click** on **OK**. The Style dialog box will disappear and the worksheet will appear with the "totals" style applied to the highlighted cells.

6. **Click anywhere** on the worksheet to remove the highlighting.

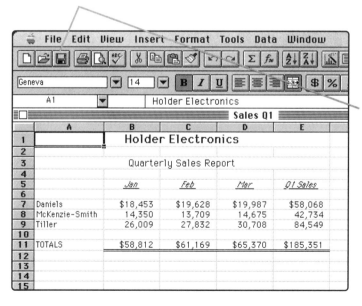

Your worksheet should now look like the example to the left.

7. **Click** on the **Save button** to save your work.

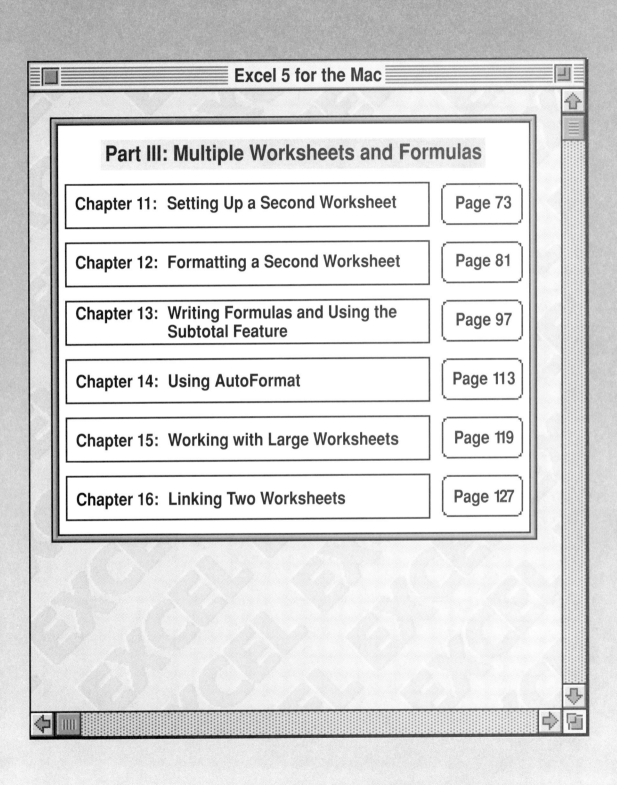

**Excel 5 for the Mac**

## Part III: Multiple Worksheets and Formulas

# Setting Up a Second Worksheet

Workbook files come with 16 tabs. Each tab represents a new worksheet. You can have up to 255 tabs in a single workbook. Can you imagine needing 255 tabs?! Tabs allow you to switch back and forth between worksheets. You can copy information from one worksheet to another. In this chapter, you will do the following:

❖ Add a second worksheet to a file
❖ Switch back and forth between two worksheets
❖ Copy data from one worksheet and paste it into a second worksheet
❖ Place names on worksheet tabs

## ADDING A SECOND WORKSHEET

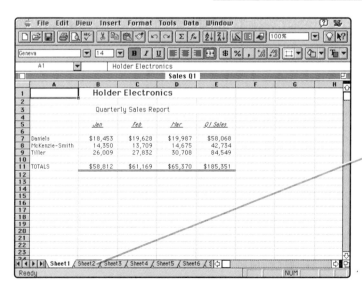

Because Excel workbooks are set up with 16 worksheets, you don't have to do anything to create additional worksheets. You simply click on the next tab.

1. **Click** on the **tab** for **Sheet2**. You will move to a blank worksheet.

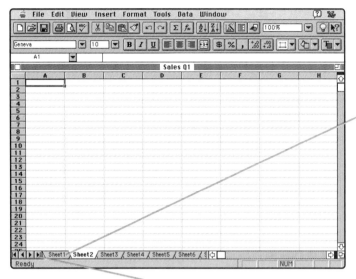

# SWITCHING BETWEEN WORKSHEETS

1. **Click** on the **Sheet1 tab**. You will go back to the Quarterly Sales Report worksheet.

You can move just as quickly through the entire 16 worksheets.

2. **Click** on the **outside right arrow** to move to the last tab in the workbook. Tabs for Sheets 12 through 16 will show at the bottom of your screen. (The outside arrows with the lines move you to the first and last tabs in the workbook. The inside arrows move you one tab at a time from where you are.)

3. **Click** on the **outside left arrow** to show Sheet1.

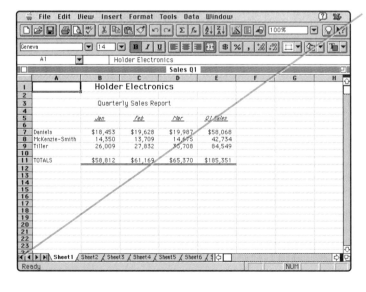

# COPYING BETWEEN WORKSHEETS

In this example, you will copy the heading from Sheet1 to Sheet2 using the Copy and Paste buttons.

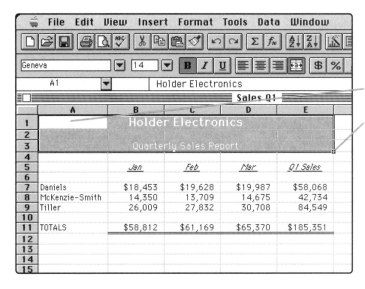

## Using the Copy Button

1. **Click** on **A1** on Sheet1.

2. **Press and hold** the mouse button and **drag** the highlight bar to **E3**.

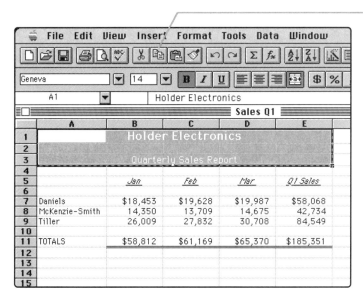

3. **Click** on the **Copy button** on the toolbar. You will see a moving border (sometimes affectionately called "running ants") around the highlighted text. The highlighted text has been copied to the Clipboard, a storage area that holds copied, deleted, or cleared data. The data will stay in the Clipboard until it is replaced with other data.

# Using the Paste Button

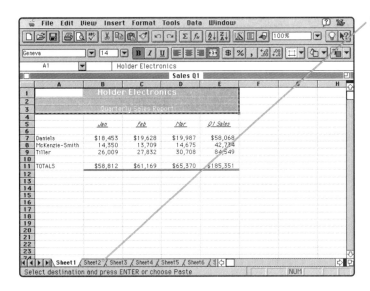

1. **Click** on the **Sheet2 tab**.

2. **Click** on **A1** on Sheet2 if it isn't already selected.

3. **Click** on the **Paste button** on the toolbar. The copied information will appear on Sheet2 beginning at cell A1.

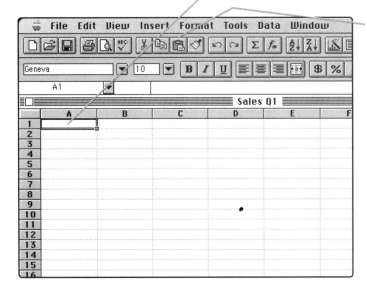

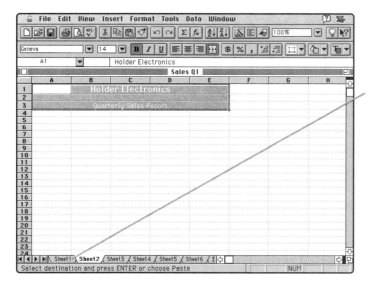

This heading is not exactly right for this worksheet. You will edit it in the next chapter.

**4. Click** on the **Sheet1 tab** to go back to Quarterly Sales Report.

# Copying with the Shortcut Menu

In this example, you will copy the salespeople's names from Sheet1 using a shortcut menu.

1. Notice that the ants are still running. **Press** the **Esc** key on your keyboard and they'll disappear.

2. **Click** on Daniels in **A7**. Keep the pointer in the middle of the cell.

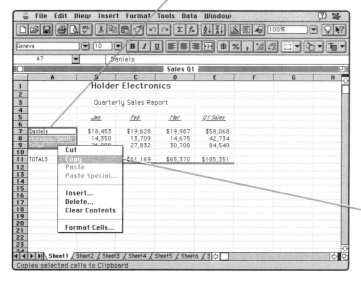

3. **Press and hold** the mouse button and **drag** the pointer down to Tiller in **A9**. All three names will be highlighted. Leave the pointer in the highlighted area.

4. **Press and hold** the **Control key** as you **press** the **mouse button**. A shortcut menu will appear.

5. **Drag** the pointer to **Copy**. The ants will appear again as the highlighted names are copied to the Clipboard.

# Pasting with
# the Shortcut Menu

1. **Click** on the **Sheet2 tab**.

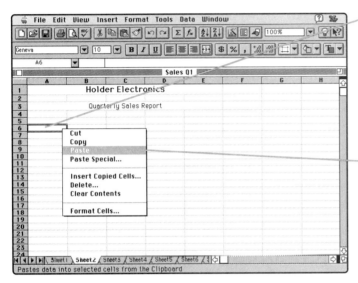

2. **Click** on **A6** on Sheet2. Leave the pointer in the cell.

3. **Press and hold** the **Control key** as you **press** the **mouse button**. A shortcut menu will appear.

4. **Drag** the mouse pointer to **Paste**. The copied names will appear beginning in A6.

5. **Increase the width** of column **A** to accommodate the long name.

6. **Click anywhere** on the worksheet to remove the highlighting.

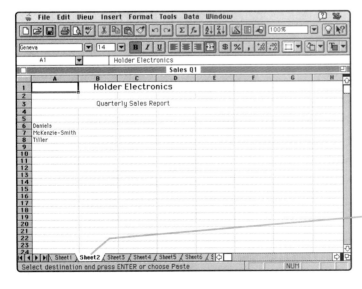

# NAMING
# WORKSHEETS

You can put a worksheet name on each tab so that it's easier to remember what each worksheet is about. The name can have up to 31 characters, including spaces.

1. **Click twice** on the **Sheet2 tab**. A Rename Sheet dialog box will appear.

2. **Type JanComm** (for January Commission). It will replace the highlighted Sheet2.

3. **Click** on **OK**. "JanComm" will appear on the Sheet2 tab.

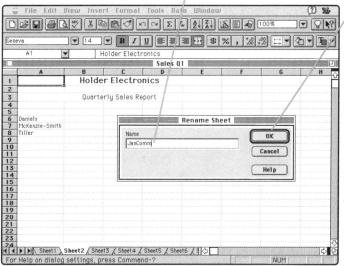

4. **Click** on the **Sheet1 tab** to make it the active worksheet. Now that Sheet1 is the active worksheet, you are ready for the next step.

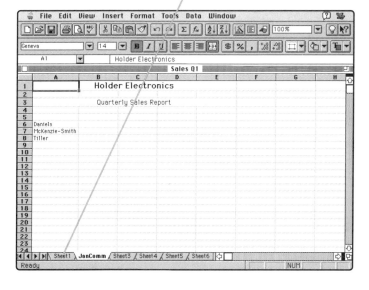

Notice that the salespeople's names are still highlighted and surrounded by the moving border.

5. **Click anywhere** on the worksheet to remove the highlighting and **press** the **Esc key** to remove the running ants.

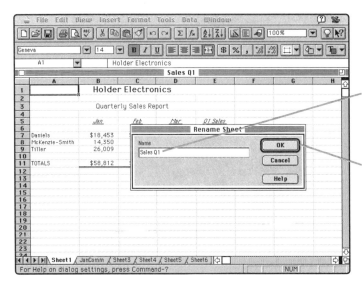

6. **Click twice** on the **Sheet1 tab**. A Rename Sheet dialog box will appear.

7. **Type Sales Q1**. It will replace the highlighted Sheet1.

8. **Click** on **OK**. "Sales Q1" will appear on the Sheet1 tab.

9. **Click** on the **Save button** on the toolbar. Both Sales Q1 and JanComm will be saved in the Sales Q1 workbook.

You will format the JanComm worksheet in the next chapter, "Formatting a Second Worksheet."

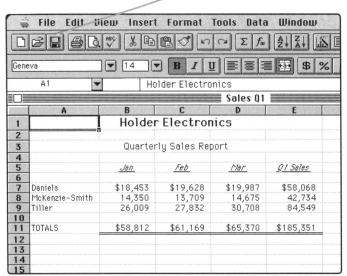

# Formatting a Second Worksheet

You can preformat an entire worksheet so that numbers appear in a specified style. In addition to the standard Macintosh functions of copying and pasting, Excel has a feature, called drag-and-drop moving, that will come in handy as you format the second worksheet. In this chapter, you will do the following:

❖ Preformat the worksheet so that all numbers appear in a specific format
❖ Move data on a worksheet with drag-and-drop moving
❖ Use text wrapping to put two lines in a cell

## EDITING COPIED DATA

In this section, you will change the report name to "January Commission Report."

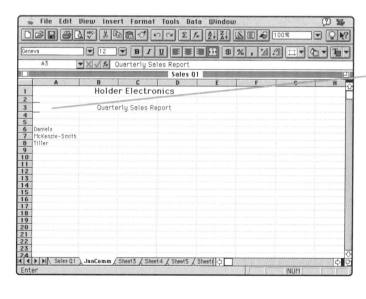

1. **Click** on the **JanComm tab** to move to that worksheet.

2. **Click twice** on **A3** to open the cell for in-cell editing. Notice that Quarterly Sales Report appears in the contents box.

3. **Place** the cursor at the **beginning** of the cell. It will change to an I-beam.

4. **Press and hold** the mouse button and **drag** the highlight bar over **Quarterly Sales**. Make sure that you don't highlight the space after "Sales" or you will delete the space between the words when you make the correction.

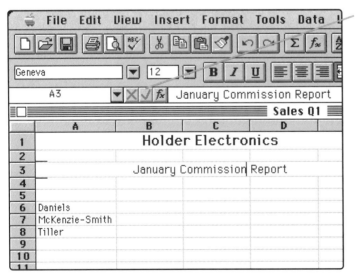

5. **Type January Commission**. It will replace the highlighted text.

6. **Click** on ✔ (or press Return) to enter the change in the cell.

# PREFORMATTING NUMBERS

In this section, you will set up the worksheet so that every number entered will appear with a comma when appropriate.

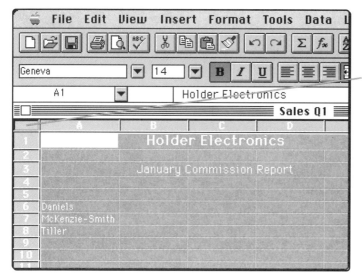

1. **Click** on the **Select All button** at the intersection of the column letters and row numbers. The entire worksheet will be highlighted in black with the exception of the first cell in the range, which will remain white.

2. **Press and hold** on **Format** in the menu bar. A pull-down menu will appear.

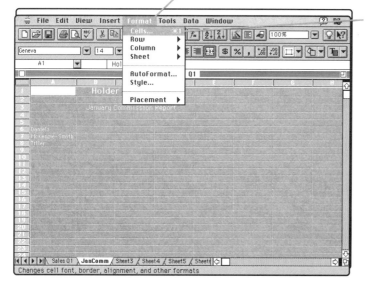

3. **Drag** the mouse pointer to **Cells**, then **release** the mouse button. The Format Cells dialog box will appear.

4. **Click** on the **Number tab** if it is not already in front.

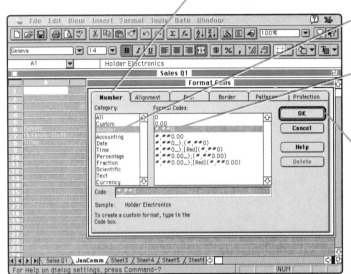

5. **Click** on **Number** in the Category box.

6. **Click** on **#,##0**, which is the third choice on the Format Codes list.

7. **Click** on **OK**. Any number entered into the worksheet will appear with a comma and no decimal places. You will modify the formatting in certain columns later in this chapter.

## DRAG-AND-DROP MOVING

If you followed the steps in Chapter 11, you copied the heading and the salespeople's names from the SalesQ1 worksheet to the JanComm worksheet. If not, you will need to follow the steps in the section "Copying Between Worksheets," beginning on page 68, before you do these procedures. In this section, you will move McKenzie-Smith and Tiller.

1. **Click** on **McKenzie-Smith** in **A7**.

2. **Move** the **pointer** to the **top border** of the cell. The pointer will become an arrow. You may have to fiddle with the placement of the pointer so that it stays an arrow.

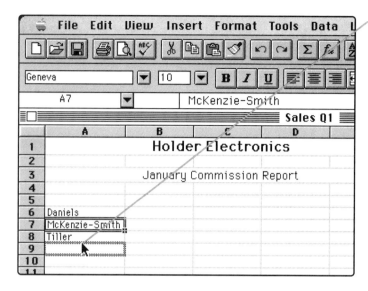

3. **Press and hold** the mouse button and **drag** McKenzie-Smith down to **A9**. You will see a gray outline being dragged.

4. **Release** the mouse button when the outline is in A9. McKenzie-Smith will appear in A9.

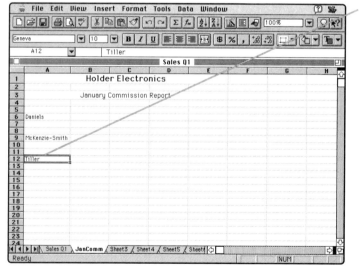

5. **Click** on Tiller in **A8** and **repeat steps 2 through 4** to move Tiller to **A12**.

# ADDING TEXT WRAPPING TO A ROW

Using the text wrapping feature allows you to divide a long entry into two lines. In this section, you will set up row 5 to wrap text so that column headings will appear as two lines.

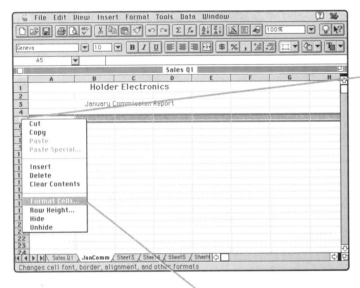

1. **Click** on the **row 5 button**. The entire row will be highlighted with the exception of the first cell, which will be white. Leave the pointer in the highlighted row.

2. **Press and hold** the **Control key** as you **press** the **mouse button**. A shortcut menu will appear.

3. **Drag** the highlight bar to **Format Cells** and **release** the mouse button. The Format Cells dialog box will appear.

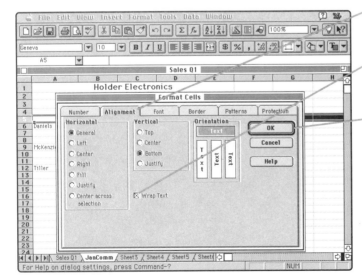

4. **Click** on the **Alignment tab** to bring it to the front.

5. **Click** on **Wrap Text** to put an X in the box.

6. **Click** on **OK**.

# Entering Column Headings

1. **Click** on **A5**.

2. **Type Salesperson. Press** the → **key** on your keyboard to enter "Salesperson" and move to B5.

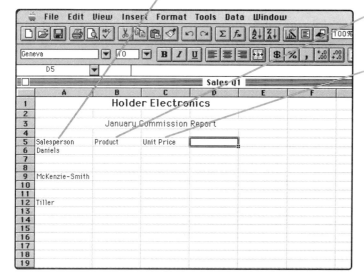

3. **Type Product** in **B5. Press** the → **key** on your keyboard.

4. **Type Unit Price. Press** the → **key** on your keyboard to move to D5.

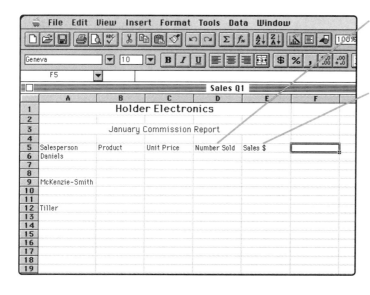

5. **Type Number Sold. Press** the → **key** on your keyboard to move to E5.

6. **Type Sales $. Press** the → **key** on your keyboard to move to F5.

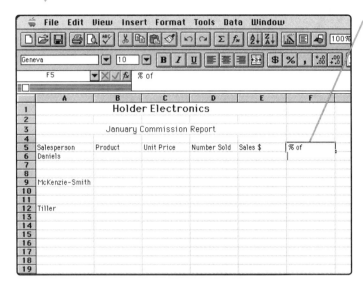

7. **Type % of.**

8. **Press and hold** the **Option key** and the ⌘ **key**. Then, press the **Return key**. This step tells Excel that you want to wrap at this exact point.

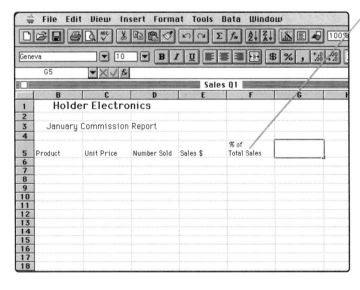

9. **Type Total Sales. Press** the → **key** on your keyboard to move to G5.

Notice that the height of row 5 has changed to fit the heading you have just entered.

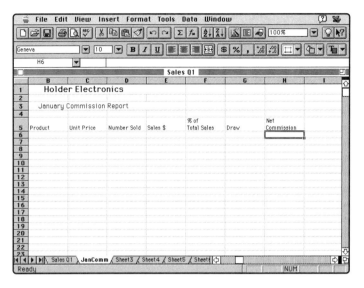

11. **Type Draw** and **press** the → **key** to move to H5.

12. **Type Net Commission** and **Press Return**.

## CHANGING MULTIPLE COLUMN WIDTHS

In this section, you will apply a single command to non-adjacent columns by using the ⌘ key when you select the columns.

1. **Click** on **B** in the **second** column heading. The entire column will be highlighted.

2. **Press and hold** the ⌘ **key** and **click** on the column heading for **E.** The entire column will be highlighted.

3. **Press and hold** the ⌘ **key** and **click** on the column heading for **G.** All three columns will be highlighted.

4. **Press and hold** on **Format** in the menu bar. A pull-down menu will appear.

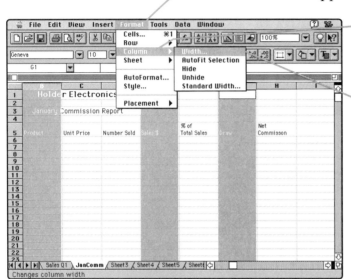

5. **Drag** the highlight bar to **Column**. A second menu will appear.

6. **Drag** the highlight bar to **Width**, then **release** the mouse button. The Column Width dialog box will appear.

7. **Type 8** in the Column Width box.

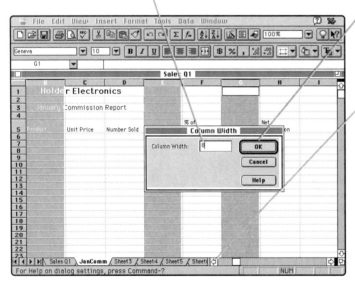

8. **Click** on **OK**. The highlighted columns will be changed to an 8-character width.

9. **Click** on the ← in the bottom scroll bar to bring column A into view if you can't see it.

# CENTERING TEXT IN A ROW

In this example, you will highlight row 5 and apply a centering command to all of the cells in the row.

1. **Click** on the **row 5 button**. The entire row will be highlighted.

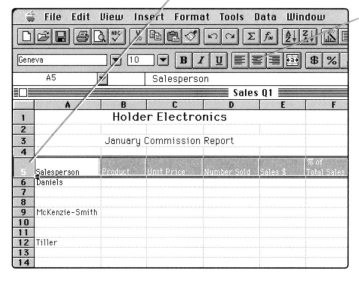

2. **Click** on the **Center button** in the toolbar. The text in each cell in row 5 will be centered.

# RECENTERING THE HEADING

Notice that the heading you copied from the first worksheet is not centered over this second worksheet. Fortunately, it's easy to fix.

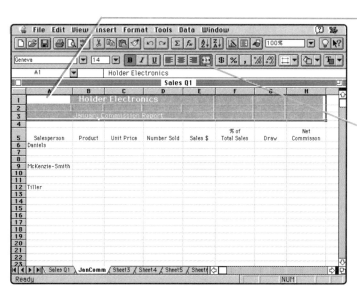

1. **Click** on **A1**.

2. **Press and hold** the mouse button and **drag** the highlight bar to **H3**.

3. **Click twice** on the **Center Across Columns button** on the toolbar. The first click will take off the centering and move the text to column A. The second click will reapply the centering command. The text will be centered across all the columns.

# REPEATING THE CONTENTS OF A CELL WITH AUTOFILL

1. **Click** on Daniels in **A6**.

2. **Click and hold** on the **Fill button** in the bottom right corner of the cell and **drag** the border down to **A8**.

3. **Release** the mouse button and "Daniels" will be repeated in all three cells.

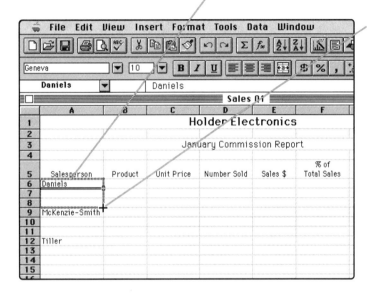

4. **Repeat steps 1 through 3** to repeat **McKenzie-Smith** in A10 and A11.

5. **Repeat steps 1 through 3** to repeat **Tiller** in A13 and A14.

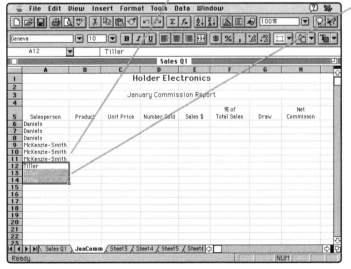

## OVERRIDING NUMBER FORMATS

Although you have preformatted the worksheet to have commas and no decimal places, you can apply a style to override this formatting. In this example, you will apply the Comma style to column C. This step will put two decimal places in the column.

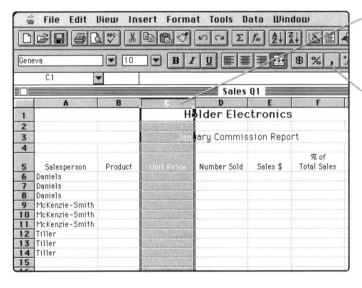

1. **Click** on the **column C button**. The entire column will be highlighted.

2. **Click** on the **Comma button** in the toolbar. You won't see any change in the screen, but the column is now formatted for two decimal places.

## COPYING AND PASTING A RANGE

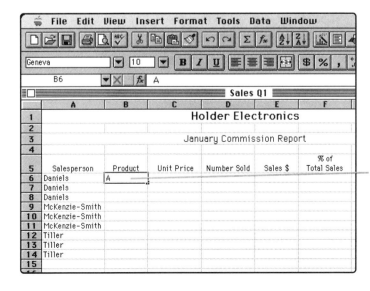

In this section, you will enter text into six cells. Then you will copy and paste the text into other cells.

## Entering Text

1. **Click** on **B6**.

2. **Type** the letter **A** and **press Return**. The border will move to B7.

3. **Repeat step 2** and **type** the letters **B** and **C** in **B7** and **B8**.

4. **Click** on **C6**.

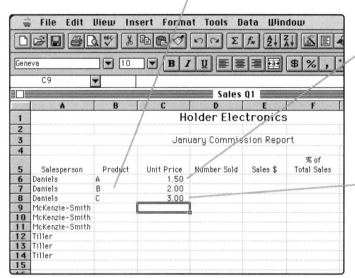

5. **Type 1.5** and **press Return**. The border will move to C7 and 1.50 will be entered into the cell because you formatted this column to have two decimal places.

6. **Repeat step 5** and **type 2** and **3** in cells **C7** and **C8**, respectively.

## Copying a Range of Cells

1. **Click** on **B6**. Leave the pointer in the middle of the cell.

2. **Press and hold** the mouse button and **drag** the pointer down to **B8** and over to **C8**. **Release** the mouse button. Leave the pointer in the highlighted area.

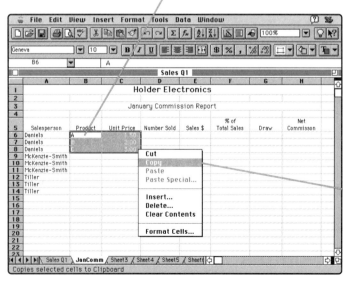

3. **Press and hold** the **Control key** as you **press** the **mouse button**. A shortcut menu will appear.

4. **Drag** the highlight bar to **Copy**, then **release** the mouse button. The highlighted cells will be surrounded by a moving border.

# Pasting a Range of Cells

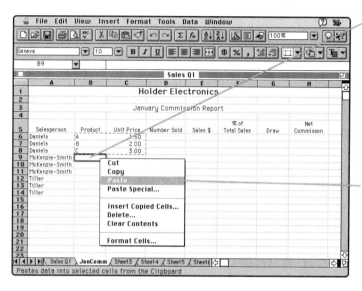

1. **Click** on **B9**. On your screen, it will be empty. Leave the pointer in the cell.

2. **Press and hold** the **Control key** as you **press** the **mouse butto**n. A shortcut menu will appear.

3. **Drag** the highlight bar to **Paste**, then **release** the mouse button. The contents of the highlighted cells will be copied into B9 through C11.

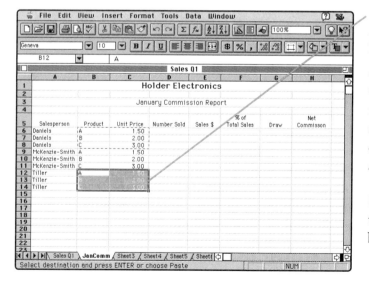

4. **Repeat steps 1 through 3** to paste the data into B12 through C14. (Because the copied data is still in the Clipboard and has not been replaced with data from another Copy or Delete command, you can paste it again.)

5. **Press** the **Esc key** to stop the running ants in the border.

# ENTERING NUMBERS

In this example, you will enter the number sold for each product.

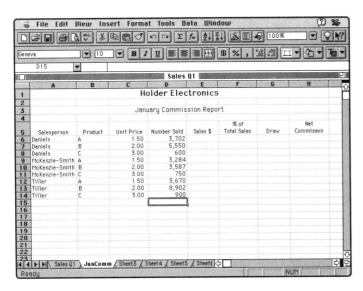

1. **Enter** the following numbers in column **D**:

**3702** in D6

**5550** in D7

**600** in D8

**3284** in D9

**3587** in D10

**750** in D11

**3670** in D12

**8902** in D13

**900** in D14

## Save Your Work

1. **Click** on the **Save button** to save your work.

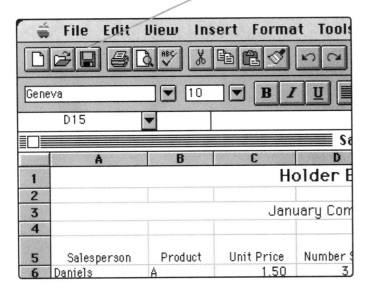

# Writing Formulas and Using the Subtotal Feature

Writing formulas is a breeze in Excel 5. You use standard symbols for mathematical processes. Addition is symbolized by a plus sign (+); subtraction by a hyphen (-); multiplication by an asterisk (*); and division by a forward slash (/). Excel 5 has an exciting new feature, called Subtotal, that will reformat your worksheet and automatically insert subtotals and a grand total. In this chapter, you will do the following:

❖ Use the Subtotal feature
❖ Write formulas for multiplication, division, subtraction, and percentage
❖ Copy formulas to other cells

## WRITING A MULTIPLICATION FORMULA

In this section, you will write a formula to calculate Sales $ = Unit Price x Number Sold.

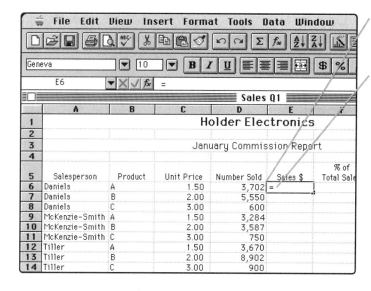

1. **Click** on **E6**. On your screen, it will be empty.

2. **Type =** to tell Excel that you are starting a formula. The = will appear in the formula bar and in the cell.

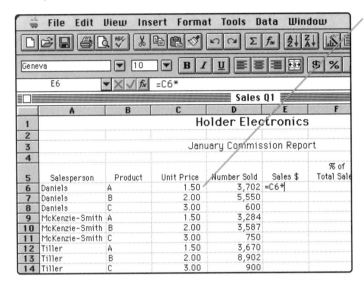

3. **Click** on 1.50 in **C6**. A running border will appear around the cell, and C6 will appear in the formula bar and in E6. (You can type a cell address into a formula, but clicking on the cell is so much easier, don't you think?)

4. **Type** * (the symbol for multiplication). The running border will disappear. The * will appear in the formula bar and in E6.

5. **Click** on **D6**. A running border will appear around the cell, and D6 will appear in the formula bar and in E6. The formula reads "=C6*D6."

6. **Click** on ✔. The results of the multiplication formula (5,553) will appear in E6.

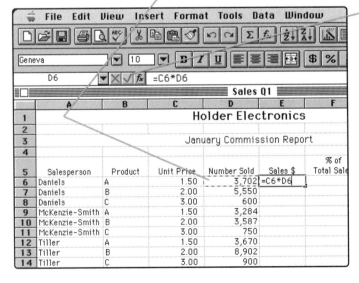

## COPYING A FORMULA

In this example, you will use the multi-talented AutoFill feature to copy the multiplication formula in E6 to the rest of the cells in the column.

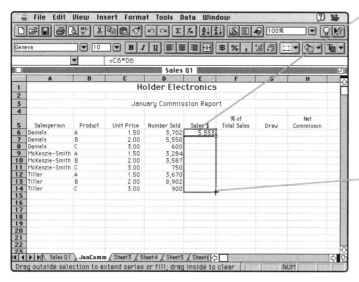

1. **Click** on **E6** if it is not already selected.

2. **Place** the **pointer** on top of the **fill handle** in the lower-right corner of the cell. The pointer will change to a black plus sign.

3. **Press and hold** the mouse button and **drag** the fill handle down the column to **E14**. You will see a gray border surround the cells.

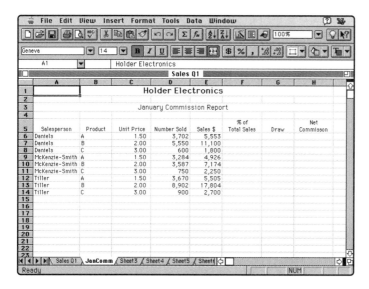

4. **Release** the mouse button when the border extends down to E14. The formula will be copied into each cell, and the resulting totals will appear.

5. **Click anywhere** on the worksheet to remove the highlighting.

# A NOTE ABOUT FORMULAS

In the previous section, you were able to copy the multiplication formula to different rows because the cells in the new rows are in the same pattern as the cells in the original row. You multiply the number in column C by the number in column D to get the answer in column E regardless of the row. When you copy this kind of formula, Excel automatically adjusts the cell reference to reflect the new row.

When you created the multiplication formula in E6, it read "=C6*D6." When you copied the formula, Excel changed the row numbers. Try the following steps to see how the cell reference changes in each row.

1. **Click twice** on E7.

Notice that the formula in the cell reads "=C7*D7" to reflect that the formula was copied into row 7.

2. **Press** the **Esc key** to remove the in-cell editing function from E7.

3. **Repeat steps 1 and 2** to see the formula in some of the other cells in column E. Each cell will have a formula that reflects the appropriate row.

# CREATING SUBTOTALS

The Subtotal feature is one of the exciting new features in Excel 5. It will automatically insert and label total rows and calculate subtotals and grand totals. To use the Subtotal feature, your data must have column labels (Salesperson, Product, or Unit Price, for example).

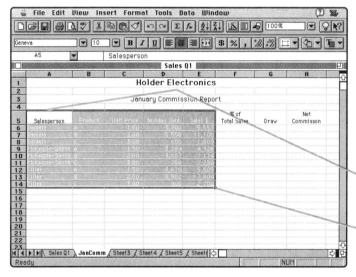

Your screen may have scrolled so that column A does not show.

1. **Click** on the ← on the bottom scroll bar to bring column A into view if you cannot see it.

2. **Click** on Salesperson in **A5**. Leave the pointer in the cell.

3. **Press and hold** the mouse button and **drag** the pointer down to **E14**. Although you can highlight all of the columns if you want Excel to put subtotals in them, in this example you will include only columns A through E.

4. **Press and hold** on **Data** in the menu bar. A pull-down menu will appear.

5. **Drag** the highlight bar to **Subtotals**, then **release** the mouse button. The Subtotal dialog box will appear.

6. **Confirm** that **Salesperson** shows in the At Each Change In box.

7. **Confirm** that **Sum** is in the Use Function box.

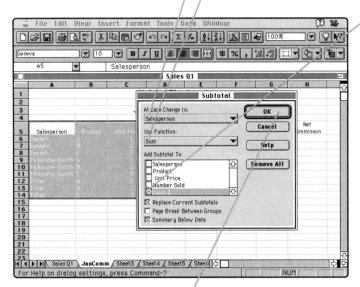

8. **Confirm** that **Sales $** has an X in the box. Sales $ is selected because this is the last column in the highlighted area. Excel automatically assumes that you want to have totals in the last column. Notice that the items in this list are your column headings. Although you can choose to have subtotals for other column headings, in this example, you will select only Sales $.

9. **Click** on **OK**. The worksheet will be reformatted.

10. **Click** on the ⬇ on the scroll bar to show row 18 on the worksheet if necessary.

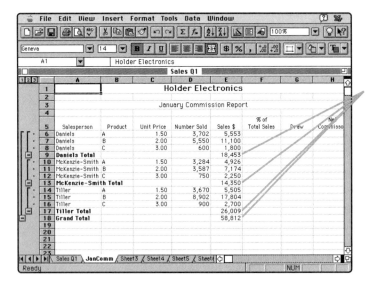

11. **Click anywhere** on the worksheet to remove the highlighting.

Notice that summary lines have been added for each salesperson and the totals automatically calculated.

# WRITING A DIVISION FORMULA

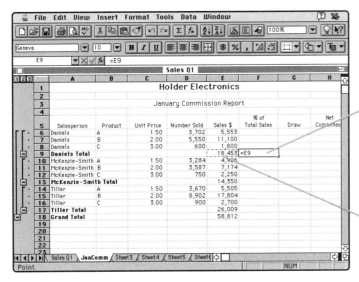

In this section, you will write a formula to calculate % of Total Sales = Salesperson's Total ÷ Grand Total.

1. **Click** on **F9**. On your screen, it will be blank.

2. **Type =** to tell Excel you are starting a formula.

3. **Click** on 18,453 in **E9**. A moving border will appear around the cell.

4. **Type /** (a forward slash), the symbol for division.

5. **Type $E$18**. Inserting the $s in the cell reference creates an *absolute cell reference*. This tells Excel it *must* use E18 as the divisor. It cannot modify this cell reference when you copy the formula.

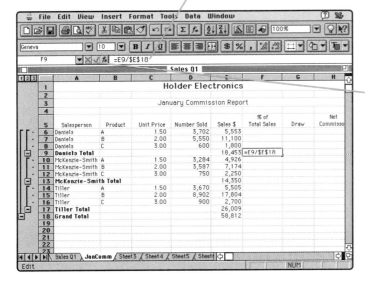

6. **Click** on the ✔. Notice that a 0 appears in F9! The worksheet is formatted for commas and no decimal places; therefore, Excel can't show the result of the formula in this cell because it is a decimal. Now you have to format the column to show a percent.

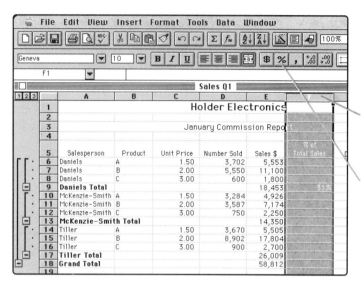

# Formatting a Column for Percents

1. **Click** on the **column F heading**. The entire column will be highlighted.

2. **Click** on the **% button** in the toolbar. "31%" will appear in F9.

# Copying a Formula with Drag and Drop

Because of the absolute cell reference, you can copy the division formula to other rows and Excel will not modify the cell reference as it did in the multiplication formula.

1. **Click** on **F9. Place** the mouse pointer on the **border of the cell**. It will change to an arrow.

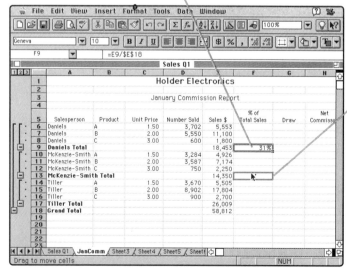

2. **Press and hold** the **Option key.** A tiny plus sign will appear, then **press and hold** the **mouse button**.

3. **Continue to hold** the **Option key** and drag the cell border to **F13.** *Release the mouse button first* then release the **Option key.** 24% will appear in F13.

4. **Repeat steps 1 through 3** to copy the formula into F17. 44% will appear in F17.

# COPYING NUMBERS

In preparation for writing the subtraction formula, you will enter the amount Daniels receives as a draw against commission and then copy that amount to the other salespeople.

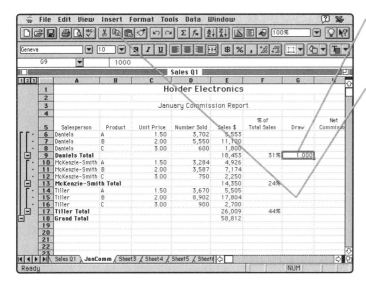

1. **Click** on **G9**.

2. **Type 1000** and **click** ✔.

3. **Click** on the **Copy button** in the toolbar. The number is now copied to the Clipboard.

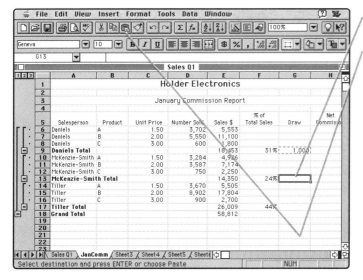

4. **Click** on **G13**.

5. **Click** on the **Paste button** in the toolbar and 1,000 will appear in G13.

6. **Repeat steps 4 and 5** to **enter 1,000** in **G17**.

7. **Press** the **Esc key** to stop the moving border around G9.

# WRITING A FORMULA WITH TWO OPERATIONS

In this section, you will write a formula to calculate Net Commission = Sales $ - Draw. This calculation requires that you multiply the Sales $ by a 15% commission and then subtract the draw amount.

1. **Click** on the ➡ on the scroll bar to bring column H into full view, if necessary.

2. **Click** on **H9**.

3. **Type =** to start a formula.

4. **Click** on 18,453 in **E9**.

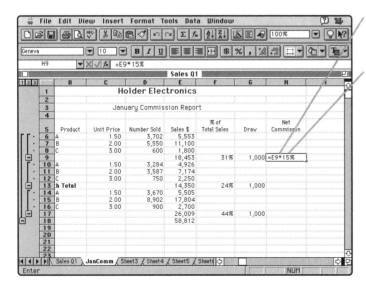

5. **Type** an **asterisk (*)**, the symbol for multiplication.

6. **Type 15%**, the percent these salespeople receive as commission. (You can enter a percent as a decimal or with the percent sign.)

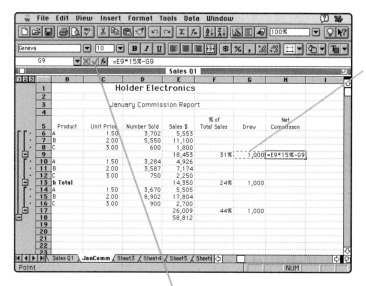

7. **Type** a **hyphen (-)**, the symbol for subtraction.

8. **Click** on 1,000 in **G9**.

9. **Click** on ✔. Excel will calculate 15% of Daniels' total sales and then subtract 1,000.

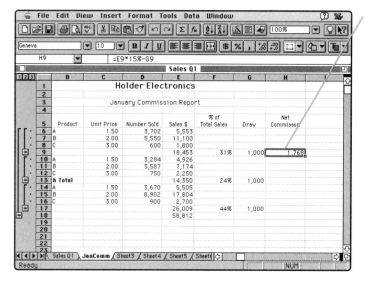

You will see 1,768 appear in H9.

You can copy this formula to other rows because the cells in the new rows are in the same pattern as the cells in row 9.

Before you copy this formula, however, there are a few details about formulas you should know.

# MORE ABOUT FORMULAS

Formulas in Excel can be as simple or as complex as you like. However, most will contain the basic arithmetic operations of addition, subtraction, multiplication, and division.

If you include more than one operation in a formula, Excel performs them in the order shown to the left.

For example, in the formula 10-2*3, the * is performed first, giving a product of 6. Then the subtraction is performed, giving a final answer of 4.

Putting parentheses in a formula will cause Excel to perform the calculation within the parentheses before all others. When a set of parentheses is inside another set of parentheses, the calculation of the inside parentheses is performed first and then the calculation required by the outside parentheses. Within parentheses, the precedence order above applies. Look at the order in which the functions are performed in the following example:

| Arithmetic operations are performed in the following order: |
| --- |
| 1. * Multiplication |
| 2. / Division |
| 3. + Addition |
| 4. – Subtraction |

325 + ((500 + B7) * 4) / 8 - E25

    |     |   |   |   |

4th      1st   2nd  3rd 5th

This example has spaces added simply to make the explanation easier to see. When you write formulas, do not put spaces before or after the operation symbols.

Consult the *User's Guide* that came with your software for a thorough discussion of formulas.

# Copying the Formula

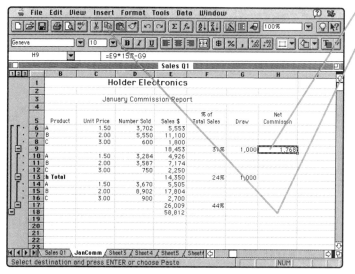

1. **Click** on **H9**.

2. **Click** on the **Copy button** in the toolbar. The selected cell will be surrounded by running ants.

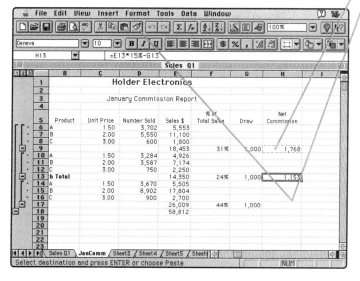

3. **Click** on **H13**.

4. **Click** on the **Paste button** in the toolbar. The formula will be pasted into the selected cell and 1,153 will appear.

5. **Repeat steps 3 and 4** to paste the formula into H17. You will see "2,901" appear in the cell.

6. **Press** the **Esc key** to stop the moving border around H9.

# USING AUTOSUM WITH NONADJACENT CELLS

In this example, you will use the AutoSum button to add the three numbers in column H.

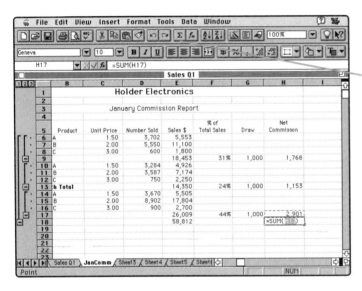

1. **Click** on **H18**. On your screen, it will be empty.

2. **Click** on the **AutoSum button (∑)** in the toolbar.

Notice that the formula in H18 is "=SUM(H17)." This means that it will add only H17 into the total. You can tell Excel to include other cells by highlighting them.

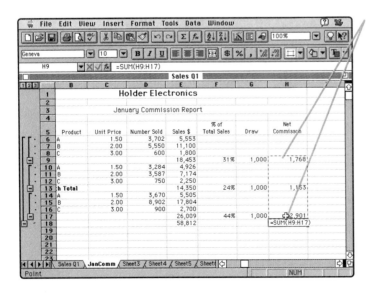

4. **Press and hold** on **H9**. **Drag** the pointer down to **H17**. Cells H9 through H17 will be surrounded by a moving border. The formula in H18 will read "=SUM(H9:H17)."

4. **Click** on ✔. The sum 5,822 will appear in H18.

# USING THE OUTLINE SYMBOLS IN SUBTOTAL

When you applied Subtotal to the JanComm worksheet, Excel added the outline symbols in the gray area to the left of the worksheet. These symbols are used to "collapse" the worksheet to show various levels of summary data.

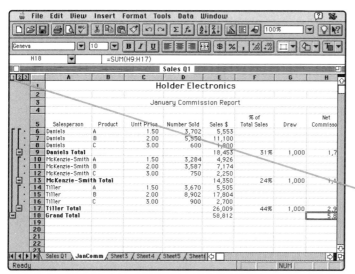

1. **Click** on the ← on the scroll bar to bring column A into view.

2. **Click** on the **level 1 outline symbol**. The worksheet will be collapsed to show only the Grand Total.

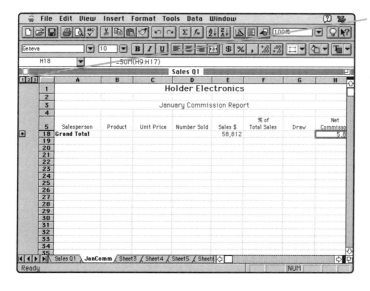

3. **Click** on the **level 2 outline symbol**. The worksheet will show only the Subtotal amounts and the Grand Total.

4. **Click** on the **level 3 outline symbol**. The worksheet will be fully expanded.

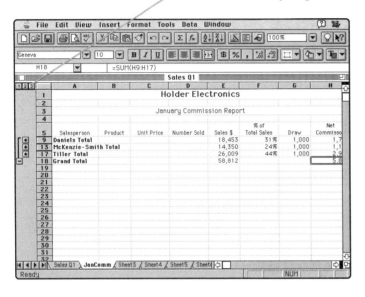

Your worksheet will look like this example.

## Save Your Work

1. **Click** on the **Save button** in the toolbar to save your work.

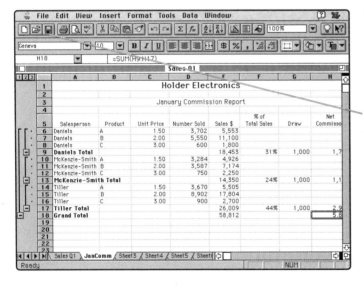

# Using AutoFormat

AutoFormat is another of Excel's special features. It contains a selection of predesigned formats you can apply to your worksheet. You can even modify an AutoFormat style. In this chapter, you will do the following:

❖ Apply an AutoFormat style
❖ Remove an AutoFormat style
❖ Modify the predesigned style

## SELECTING AN AUTOFORMAT STYLE

In this section, you will choose an AutoFormat style and apply it to the JanComm worksheet. In this example, you will not change the style of the heading; therefore, you will not include it in the range of cells to be styled.

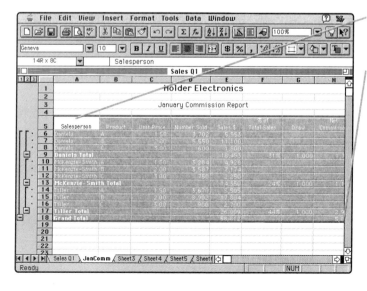

1. **Click** on **A5**. Leave the pointer in the cell.

2. **Press and hold** the mouse button and **drag** the highlight bar over to **H5** and down to **H18**. **Release** the mouse button when rows 5 through 18 are highlighted.

3. **Press and hold** on **Format** in the menu bar. A pull-down menu will appear.

4. **Drag** the highlight bar to **AutoFormat**, then **release** the mouse button. The Auto-Format dialog box will appear.

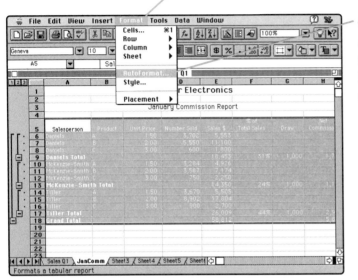

The AutoFormat dialog box contains a list of 16 formats you can apply to your worksheet.

As you click on each choice in the Table Format list, the Sample box will show what the format looks like. Click on a few of the choices to see what they look like. After you've seen the selections, go on to step 5.

5. **Click** on **Classic 2**.

6. **Click** on **Options**. The AutoFormat dialog box will be expanded to include Formats to Apply.

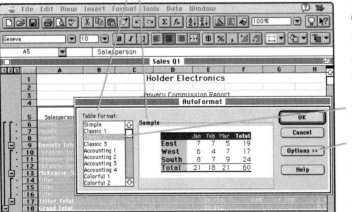

# CUSTOMIZING AN AUTOFORMAT STYLE

If you like a particular AutoFormat style, you can customize it so that it doesn't override any formatting you have already applied to your worksheet.

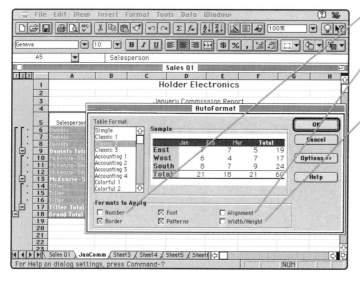

1. **Click** on **Number** to remove the ✕ from the box.

2. **Click** on **Alignment** to remove the ✕ from the box.

3. **Click** on **Width/Height** to remove the ✕ from the box.

The number formatting, alignment, and width and height of cells will now remain as you set them, even after the Classic2 style is applied to the worksheet.

4. **Click** on **OK**. The dialog box will close and the Classic2 style will be applied to the worksheet.

The color on the worksheet is a little strange, but it will change when you remove the highlighting.

5. **Click anywhere** on the worksheet to remove the highlighting.

# REMOVING AN AUTOFORMAT STYLE

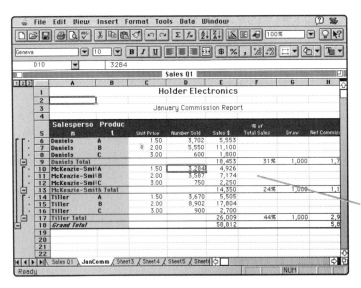

You can use the Undo button to remove an AutoFormat style if you use it immediately after you apply the style. If you have performed any other function, however, you will have to do the following steps to remove the AutoFormat style.

1. **Click anywhere** in the formatted range of cells.

2. **Press and hold** on **Format** in the menu bar. A pull-down menu will appear.

3. **Drag** the highlight bar to **AutoFormat**, then **release** the mouse button. The AutoFormat dialog box will appear.

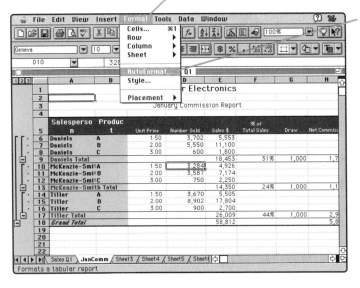

4. **Click and hold** the **button** on the scroll bar and **drag** it down to the bottom of the scroll bar.

5. **Click** on **None**.

6. **Click** on **OK**. The worksheet will reappear with the AutoFormat style removed.

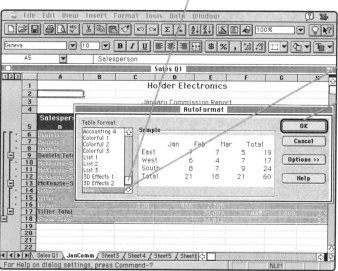

Notice that this step removed all the styles from the worksheet. You can reapply the styles or you can do the following step:

7. **Click** on the **Undo button** in the toolbar. The Classic2 AutoFormat style will be restored.

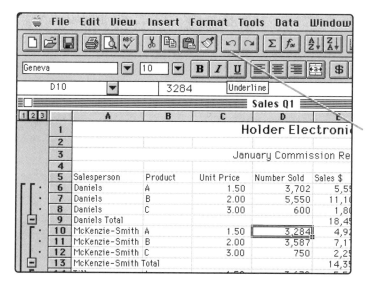

# MODIFYING AN APPLIED AUTOFORMAT STYLE

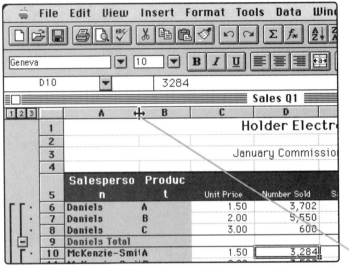

You modify an applied AutoFormat style the same way you apply any style to a cell, column, or row. In this example, you will increase the width of column A automatically and column B manually.

## Increasing Cell Width Automatically

1. **Place** the mouse pointer on the **line between the column A and column B headers**. The pointer will change to the shape you see in this example.

2. **Click twice**. The column will expand to a best-fit width.

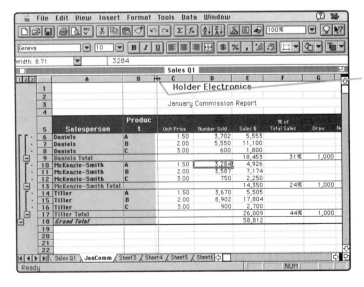

## Increasing Cell Width Manually

1. **Place** the mouse pointer on the **line between the column B and column C headers**.

2. **Press and hold** the mouse button and **drag** the line to the right to expand the column. **Release** the mouse button when the column is wide enough.

# Working with Large Worksheets

When you work with a large worksheet, it is annoying to watch the column and row headings scroll out of sight. Excel solves this problem by letting you freeze parts of your worksheet into separate sections, or panes, which always remain in view. It also lets you change the view so that more of your worksheet is visible on your screen. In this chapter, you will do the following:

❖ Freeze and unfreeze a row and column (panes)
❖ Change the view (zoom out) so that you can see more of the worksheet on your screen
❖ Zoom in to magnify a portion of the worksheet

## FREEZING COLUMNS AND ROWS

In this section, you will freeze the JanComm worksheet so that row 5 and columns A and B are always visible. Because you do not need to have "Holder Electronics" and "January Commission Report" on your screen at all times, you can scroll these names out of sight before you freeze the worksheet.

1. **Click** on the ⬇ on the scroll bar until rows 1 through 4 have scrolled out of sight, as you see in this example.

# Selecting the Freezing Point

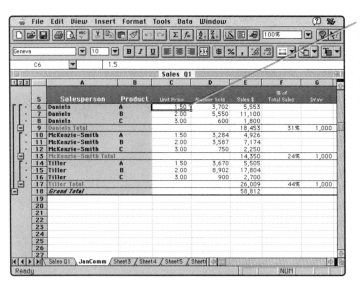

1. **Click** on **C6**. This will become the freezing point and cells above it and to the left of it will stay frozen on your screen.

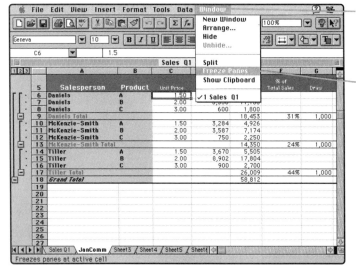

2. **Press and hold** on **Window** in the menu bar. A pull-down menu will appear.

3. **Drag** the highlight bar to **Freeze Panes**, then **release** the mouse button.

Notice the freeze lines on the worksheet. The horizontal line is hard to see because of the colored heading, but it's there.

## Scrolling in a Frozen Worksheet

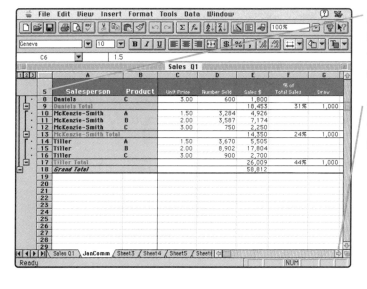

1. **Click twice** on the ⬇ on the scroll bar to scroll down the worksheet.

Notice that the headings in row 5 remain in view even though rows 6 and 7 have scrolled out of sight.

2. **Click twice** on the ➡ on the bottom scroll bar to scroll to the right in the worksheet.

Notice that columns A and B remain on your screen even though columns C and D have scrolled out of sight.

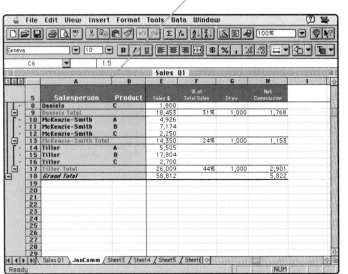

## UNFREEZING PANES

It doesn't matter where the selected cell is when you unfreeze panes. You will be returned to the "freezing point," which in this example is C6.

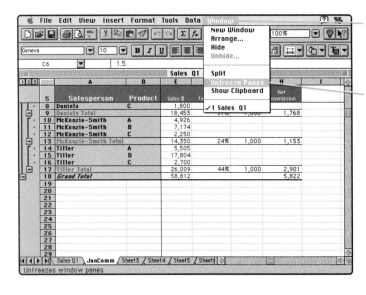

1. **Press and hold** on **Window** in the menu bar. A pull-down menu will appear.

2. **Drag** the highlight bar to **Unfreeze Panes**, then **release** the mouse button. The freeze lines will be removed from the worksheet.

# CHANGING THE SCREEN VIEW

The Zoom feature in Excel resembles the zoom lens on a camera. You can zoom out and fit more of the worksheet on the screen. Or you can zoom in and magnify a specific area.

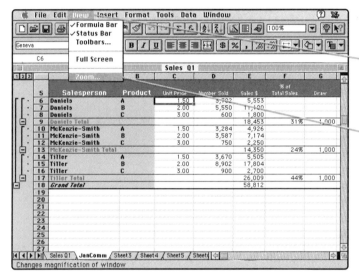

# Zooming Out

1. **Press and hold** on **View** in the menu bar. A pull-down menu will appear.

2. **Drag** the highlight bar to **Zoom**, then **release** the mouse button. The Zoom dialog box will appear.

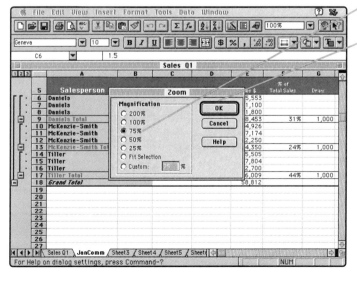

3. **Click** on **75%**.

4. **Click** on **OK**. You will zoom out to a view where the worksheet has shrunk to 75% of its normal size.

# Zooming In

1. **Press and hold** on **View** in the menu bar. A pull-down menu will appear.

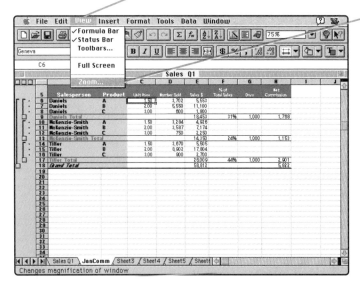

2. **Drag** the highlight bar to **Zoom**, then **release** the mouse button. The Zoom dialog box will appear.

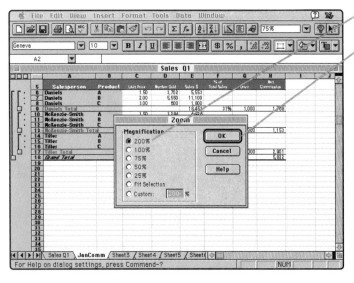

3. **Click** on **200%**.

4. **Click** on **OK**. The worksheet will appear at 200% of its normal size.

# Returning to the Normal View

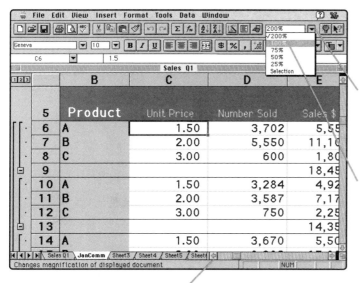

Excel has a button in the toolbar that makes changing views easy.

1. **Press and hold** on the ▼ to the right of the Zoom Control box. A drop-down list will appear.

2. **Drag** the highlight bar to **100%**, then **release** the mouse button. The screen will return to the normal view.

If column A is hidden, click on the ◄ on the bottom scroll bar until column A comes into view.

# Linking Two Worksheets

When you establish a link between two worksheets, any change made in the linked data on the first worksheet (the source worksheet) is immediately reflected in the linked data on the second worksheet (the dependent worksheet). The process of creating a link is very easy. In this chapter, you will do the following:

❖ Use JanComm as the source worksheet and open a new file as the dependent worksheet
❖ Arrange both worksheets on your screen at the same time
❖ Link the worksheets
❖ Test the link

## GETTING READY TO LINK

In this section, you will use JanComm as the source worksheet because it contains the net commission data that will be transferred to a second worksheet. Next, you will open a new file that will become the dependent worksheet and receive the data from the source worksheet. Open the Sales Q1 workbook and go to the JanComm worksheet, if you are not already there.

## Opening a New Workbook

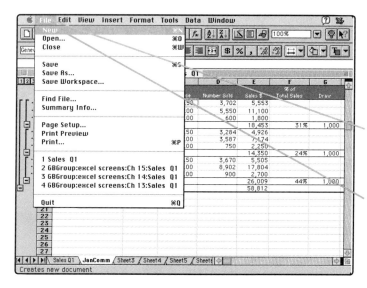

1. **Press and hold** on **File** in the menu bar. A pull-down menu will appear.

2. **Drag** the highlight bar to **New,** then **release** the mouse button. A new workbook will appear and cover up the Sales Q1 workbook.

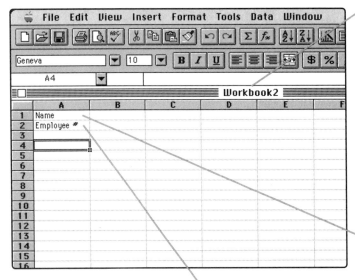

Notice Workbook2 in the title bar.

# Entering Data in the New Workbook

1. **Click** on **A1**, if it is not already selected. On your screen, it will be blank.

2. **Type Name** and **press Return**.

3. **Type Employee #** in A2 and **press Return twice** to move to A4.

4. **Type Month** and **press Return** to move to A5.

# Entering a Series of Months

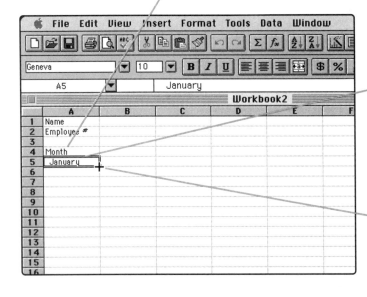

In this section, you will enter a series of months in Column A.

1. **Press** the **spacebar twice** and then **type January**. This step will indent "January" two spaces.

2. **Click** on ✔.

3. **Place** the pointer on the **fill handle** in the lower right corner of the cell border. It will become a black plus sign.

4. **Press and hold** the mouse button and **drag** the fill handle down to **A16**. The bottom border of the cell will expand as you drag.

5. **Release** the mouse button when you have included A5:A16 in the border outline. The series January through December will appear in the cells. Notice that the entire series is indented two spaces. If you dragged too far down column A and the series started to repeat itself, simply drag the fill handle up to remove the extra months.

6. **Click anywhere** to remove the highlighting.

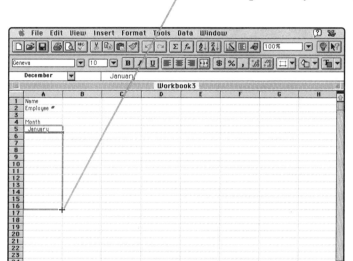

## Entering a Number as Text

In this section, you will enter a name and employee number for Stacey Tiller. Because the employee number is for identification purposes only, you don't want Excel to treat it as an actual number. If you type an apostrophe before the number, Excel will treat it as text. The number will appear aligned on the left in the cell, like other text.

1. **Click** on **B1**. On your screen, it will be empty.

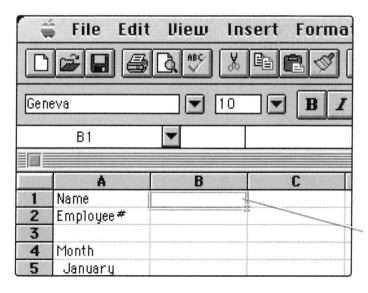

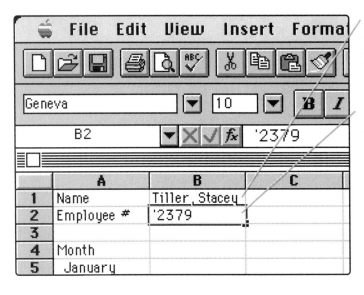

2. **Type Tiller, Stacey** and **press** the **Return key** on your keyboard to enter the name in the cell and move to B2.

3. **Type '2379**. Don't forget the apostrophe. Press **Return** to enter the number and move to the next cell.

## Formatting the Worksheet

In this section, you will format the worksheet to have commas and two decimal places.

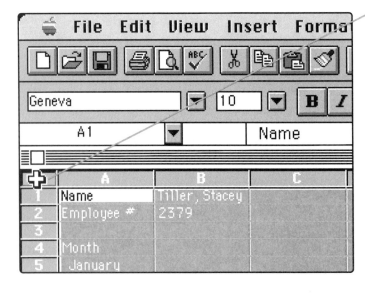

1. **Click** on the **Select All button** at the intersection of the row and column headings. The entire worksheet will be highlighted.

2. **Press and hold** on **Format** in the menu bar. A pull-down menu will appear.

3. **Drag** the highlight bar to **Cells**, then **release** the mouse button. The Format Cells dialog box will appear.

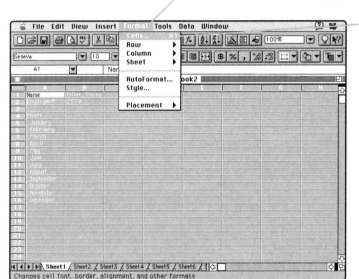

4. **Click** on the **Number tab** to bring it to the front if it is not already there.

5. **Click** on **Number** in the Category list.

6. **Click** on **#,##0.00**, which is the fourth option in the Format Codes list.

7. **Click** on **OK**. The dialog box will close. Any number entered into this worksheet will appear with a comma and two decimal places.

8. When the worksheet appears, **click anywhere** to remove the highlighting.

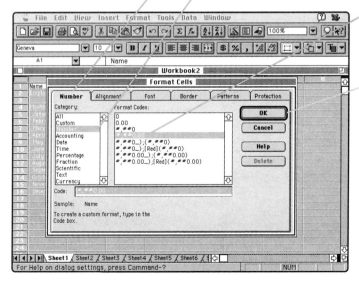

# SWITCHING BETWEEN FILES

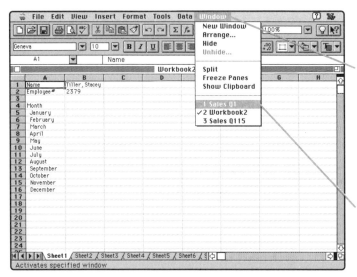

You can easily move back and forth between open files.

1. **Press and hold** on **Window** in the menu bar. A pull-down menu will apprear.

Notice that the pull-down menu lists all open files at the bottom.

2. **Drag** the highlight bar to **Sales Q1** and **release** the mouse button. Sales Q1 will come to the foreground on your screen.

# SHOWING TWO FILES AT THE SAME TIME

Now that the new worksheet is formatted, you are ready to make the link. The easiest way to begin linking two worksheets is to first arrange them on your screen so you can see them both at the same time. This, however, is not a prerequisite to linking.

1. **Press and hold** on **Window** in the menu bar. A pull-down menu will appear.

2. **Drag** the highlight bar to **Arrange**, and **release** the mouse button. The Arrange Windows dialog box will appear.

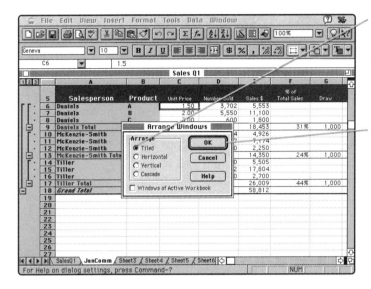

3. **Click** on **Tiled** if it does not already have a dot in the circle. This step will make the files appear side by side on the screen.

4. **Click** on **OK**.

The file that was visible on your screen when you performed the Tile command is the active file in the tile arrangement. The active window has lines in the title bar.

# MAKING THE LINK

Making the actual link between worksheets is the easiest part of the process.

1. **Click** repeatedly on the ➡ on the scroll bar of SALESQ1 until you can see column H.

2. **Click** on 2,901 in **H17**.

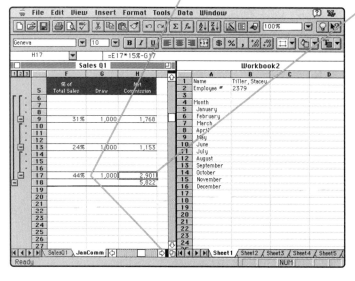

3. **Press and hold** on **Edit** in the menu bar. A pull-down menu will appear.

4. **Drag** the highlight bar to **Copy** and **release** the mouse button. The contents of the cell will be copied to the Clipboard, and you will see the running ants.

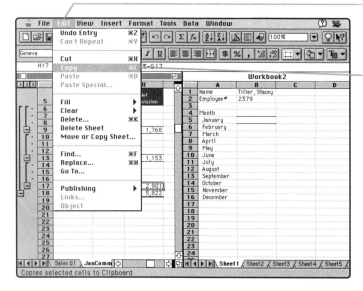

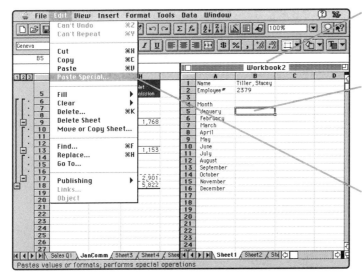

5. **Click** on the **Workbook2 title bar** to make it the active worksheet.

6. **Click** on **B5**.

7. **Press and hold** on **Edit** in the menu bar. A pull-down menu will appear.

8. **Drag** the highlight bar to **Paste Special** and **release** the mouse button.

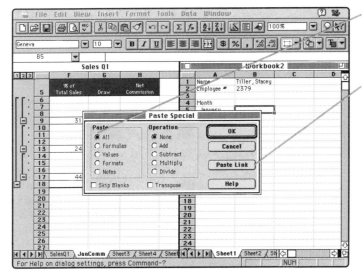

9. **Click** on **All** if it does not already have a dot in the circle.

10. **Click** on **Paste Link**. The dialog box will close and the number from the first worksheet will be linked to the second worksheet.

Notice that the number appears with two decimal places although it had no decimal places on the source worksheet. The reason is that you formatted the dependent worksheet to have two decimal places. When the format of the source and dependent worksheets are different, the format of the dependent worksheet controls the appearance of the data in the dependent worksheet.

The equal sign (=) at the beginning of the formula bar tells you that this cell is the result of a formula. [Sales Q1] in the formula bar shows that this cell is the result of a formula in the Sales Q1 workbook. JanComm tells you the worksheet name. The exclamation point (!) means that it is a linked cell. The dollar signs ($H$17) indicate that Excel will always look in this specific cell in the source worksheet for the data to link to the dependent worksheet. This is called an *absolute cell reference*.

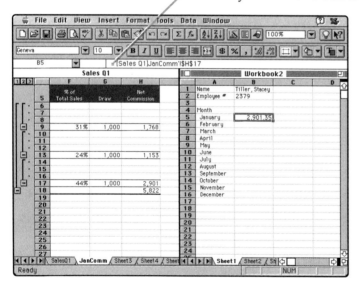

In the next section, you will have a little fun and test the link. You can do this by changing the Net Commission amount on Sales Q1 and then watching the change reflected in the linked data in the dependent worksheet. However, you cannot simply change the Net Commission amount because it is the result of a formula. You must change one of the numbers that is part of the formula. Then the Net Commission amount will change. It gets a little complicated, doesn't it?

# TESTING THE LINK

In this section, you will change the Draw amount on the source worksheet and watch as it affects the data in the dependent worksheet.

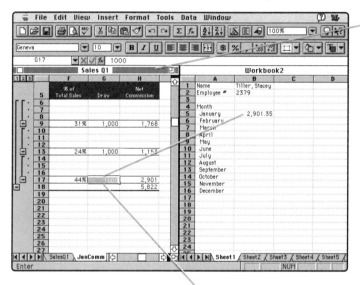

1. **Click** on the **title bar** of the Sales Q1 worksheet to make it the active worksheet.

2. **Click twice** on **G17** to open the cell for in-cell editing. On your screen 1,000 will be in G17.

3. **Click twice** again to highlight the contents of the cell.

4. **Type 500** and **press Return** to insert the new number into G17. Watch as B5 on the new worksheet changes to 3,401.35.

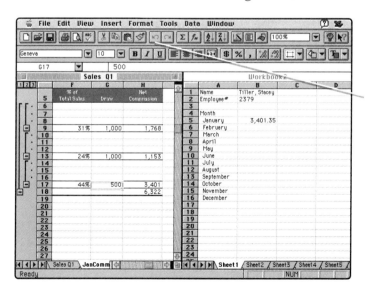

## Undoing the Change

1. **Click** on the **Undo button** in the toolbar to undo the change. The original numbers will appear.

# CLOSING WITHOUT SAVING

Because the unnamed Workbook2 was opened only to demonstrate the linking process, you will close it without saving.

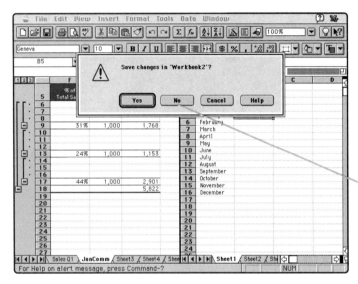

1. **Click** on the **Workbook2 title bar** to make it the active worksheet.

2. **Click** on the **Close box** (☐) in the Workbook2 title bar. The Close dialog box will appear.

3. **Click** on **No**. The file will close. Because you never saved this file, the work you did in this file is gone.

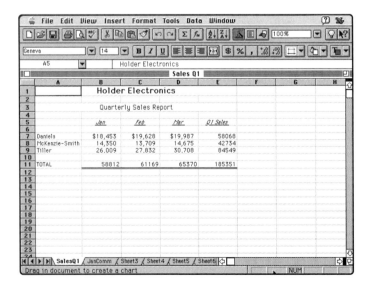

## Enlarging the Remaining File

1. **Click** on the **Zoom box** (☐) on the Sales Q1 title bar. The worksheet will be enlarged to fill the screen.

2. **Click** on the **SalesQ1 tab** in preparation for Chapter 17.

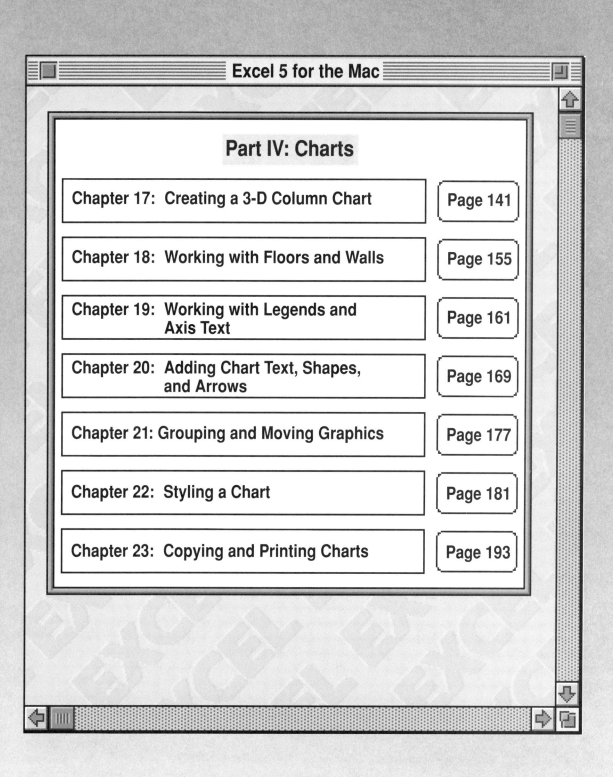

# Part IV: Charts

**Excel 5 for the Mac**

# Creating a 3-D Column Chart

With Excel 5's ChartWizard, you can create a chart (a graphic presentation of your worksheet) automatically. You can select from a number of predesigned formats, including 3-D bar, line, pie, or area charts. After the chart is created, you can easily change it to another type. In this chapter, you will do the following:

❖ Create a simple column chart using the ChartWizard
❖ Add a chart title and legend
❖ Add category and value titles
❖ Change the column chart to a 3-D column chart
❖ Change the colors of the chart's bars
❖ Save the chart with the worksheet

## USING THE CHARTWIZARD

1. **Open** the **Sales Q1 worksheet** you created in Part I and Part II. Refer to Chapter 7, "Opening a Saved Workbook," if you need help.

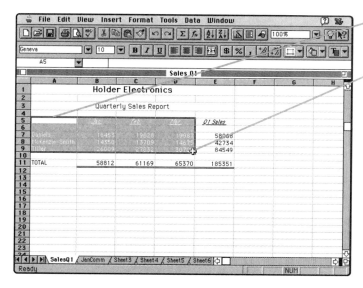

2. **Move** the mouse pointer to A5.

3. **Press and hold** the mouse button as you **drag** the **pointer** diagonally down to **D9**. **Release** the mouse button when you have highlighted the salespeoples' names and the sales data for Jan, Feb, and Mar (cells A5 through D9). Do not highlight the totals in column E and row 11.

4. **Click** on the **ChartWizard button**. If you are using Excel at work or someone has used Excel on your computer before you, it's possible that the ChartWizard tool is in another location on the toolbar.

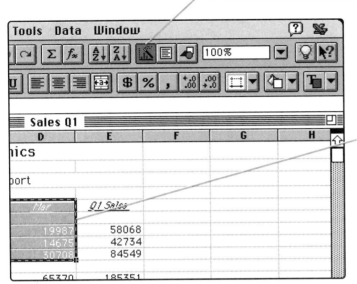

Notice that the cells you highlighted in step 3 are surrounded by a border of running ants.

5. **Place** the **pointer** in cell **A13**. (*Don't click yet.*) The pointer will become a plus sign and a tiny column chart. Line up the center of the plus sign with the top left border of the cell.

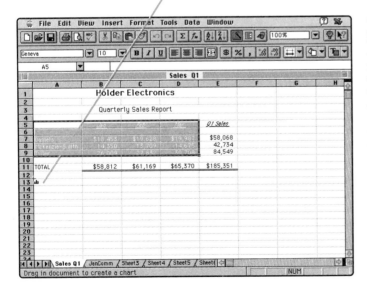

6. **Press and hold** the mouse button as you **drag** the **pointer** diagonally across to **F27**. (This process tells Excel where to place your chart.) Don't be concerned that you cannot see row 27 at first. As you drag the cursor down, the screen will automatically show more rows.

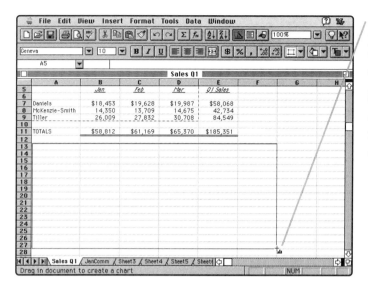

7. When cells A13 through F27 have been enclosed in the border, **release** the mouse button. The ChartWizard – Step 1 of 5 dialog box may appear in a different location from what you see in the next example.

Notice that the Range text box refers to the cells you highlighted in step 3. If the range is not correct, you can type the correct cell reference now. The correct cell range is $A$5:$D$9. This means that you have highlighted the range of cells A5 through D9.

8. **Click** on **Next**. The ChartWizard – Step 2 of 5 dialog box will appear.

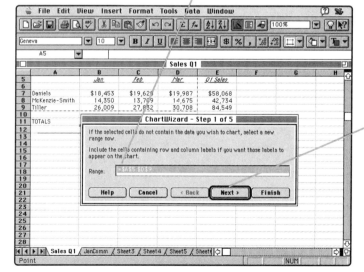

## Selecting a Column Chart

Notice the 15 different charts you can create with this dialog box.

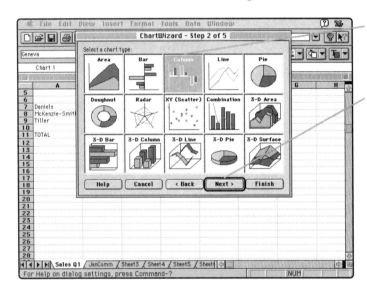

1. **Click** on the **Column chart tool** if it is not already highlighted.

2. **Click** on **Next**. The ChartWizard – Step 3 of 5 dialog box will appear.

## Selecting the Chart Format

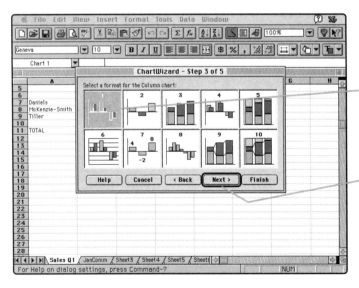

Notice the 10 different column chart formats you can create with this dialog box.

1. **Click** on the **Standard Column chart button** (selection number 1) if it is not already highlighted.

2. **Click** on **Next**. The ChartWizard – Step 4 of 5 dialog box will appear.

# Adding a Chart Title

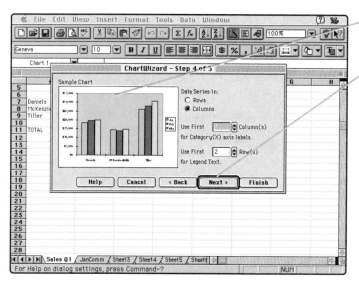

Notice the Sample Chart Preview window.

1. **Click** on **Next**. The ChartWizard – Step 5 of 5 dialog box will appear.

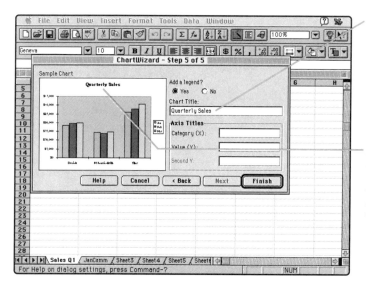

2. **Type Quarterly Sales** in the Chart Title text box. *Do not press Enter or click on Finish* until you have completed steps 1 through 5 in the following section.

Notice that after a brief pause the title "Quarterly Sales" is added to the Sample Chart preview window.

# Adding Category and Value Titles

In Excel, X and Y axes titles are called Category titles (X axis) and Value titles (Y axis). You will add the label "Top Three" to the X axis where the names of the salespeople appear and add "Dollars" to explain that the numbers on the Y-axis scale represent money.

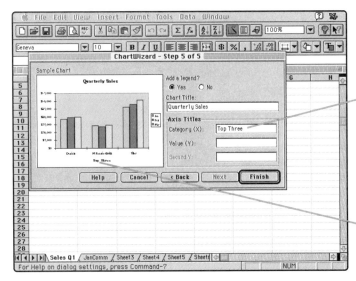

1. **Click** in the **Category (X) text box** to set the cursor in the box.

2. **Type Top Three**. *Do not press Enter or click on Finish.*

After a brief pause, Top Three will appear under the chart.

3. **Click** in the **Value (Y) text box** to set the cursor in the box.

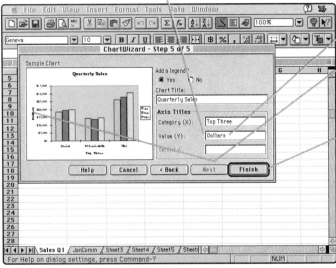

4. **Type Dollars**.

Notice that after a brief pause "Dollars" will appear on the left side of the chart.

5. **Click** on **Finish**. The Quarterly Sales report column chart will appear on your worksheet.

Congratulations! You have created an embedded column chart.

Note: An embedded chart is a permanent part of your worksheet. Whenever you make a change in your worksheet data, the change is reflected in this chart.

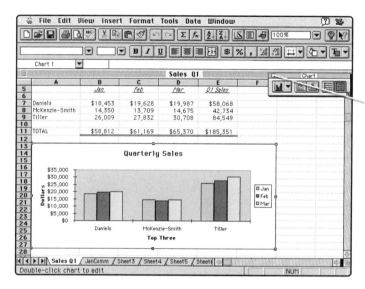

## CHANGING THE VIEW

1. **Click** on the **Control menu box** on the Chart toolbar to close it.

2. **Click** on the ⬇ on the scroll bar to bring the entire chart into view if necessary.

## MAKING A 3-D COLUMN CHART

Creating a 3-D chart is a two-step process. First you will select the 3-D chart type and then you will change the 3-D format.

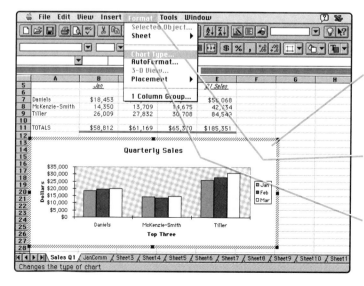

## Selecting the Chart Type

1. **Click twice anywhere** on the chart to make it active. The border of the chart will turn into a striped pattern.

2. **Press and hold** on **Format** in the menu bar. A pull-down menu will appear.

3. **Drag** the highlight bar to **Chart Type**, then **release** the mouse button. The Chart Type dialog box will appear.

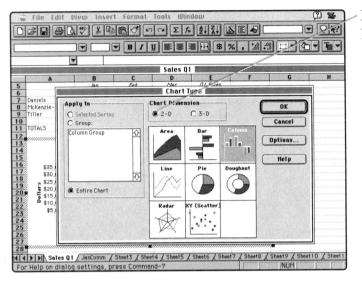

Notice that the 2-D Chart Dimension is selected.

4. **Click** on **3-D** to place a dot in the circle. Six 3-D chart type options will appear.

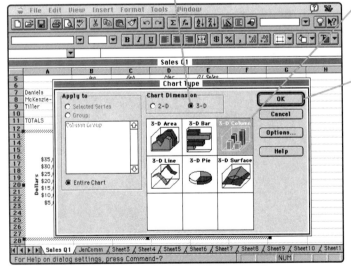

5. **Click** on the **3-D column chart option** if it is not already highlighted.

6. **Click** on **OK**. The chart will reappear. Don't panic when you see it. You will quickly fix its weird look in the next section.

# Selecting the 3-D Format

This is weird looking. Don't worry. You can fix it.

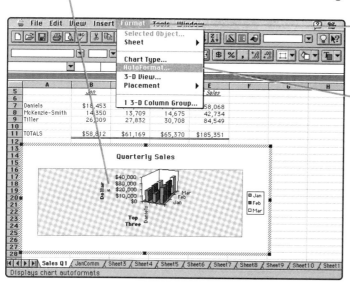

1. **Press and hold** on **Format** in the menu bar. A pull-down menu will appear.

2. **Drag** the highlight bar to **AutoFormat**, then **release** the mouse button. The AutoFormat dialog box will appear.

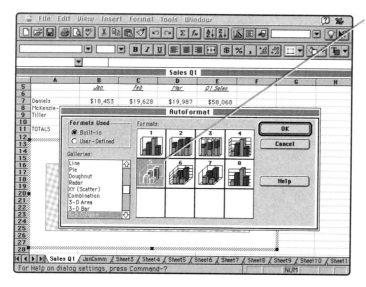

Notice that there are eight 3-D column charts and that chart number 5 is highlighted.

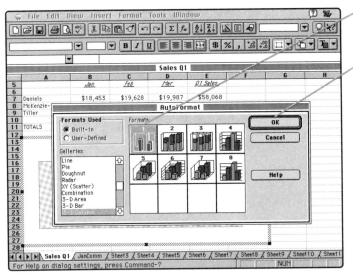

3. **Click** on the **first Chart** in the Formats box.

4. **Click** on **OK**. The Quarterly Sales Report chart will now appear in 3-D.

## Changing the Colors of the Columns

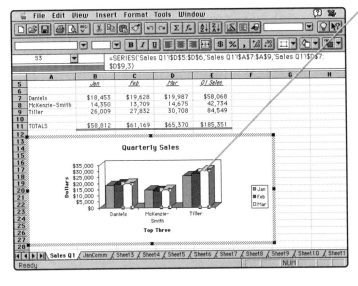

1. **Click** on the **largest Tiller column**.

Notice that the other two yellow columns are also selected and will also change.

2. **Click twice** on the **largest Tiller column**. The Format Data Series text box will appear.

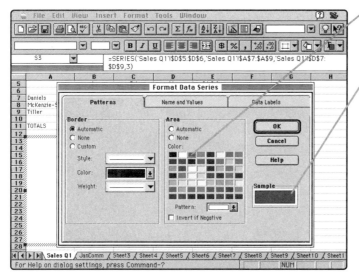

3. **Click** on the **red square**, the third from the left in the top row of the Color palette.

Notice that the color selected is shown in the Sample box.

4. **Click** on **OK**. The Quarterly Sales Report chart will appear. The columns you selected will now be red.

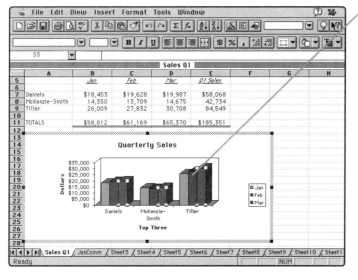

5. **Click twice** on the **middle Tiller column**. The Format Data Series text box will appear.

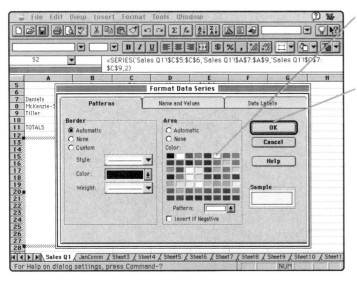

6. **Click** on the **yellow square**, third from the right on the top row of the color palette.

7. **Click** on **OK**. The Quarterly Sales Report chart will appear. The middle column will now become yellow.

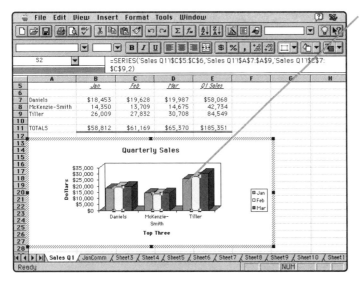

8. **Click twice** on the **shortest Tiller column**. The Format Data Series text box will appear.

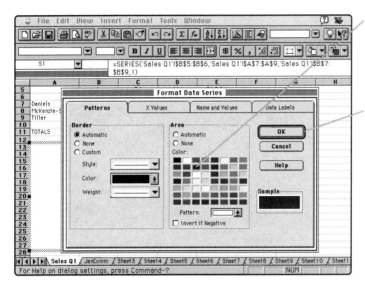

**9. Click** on the **blue square**, third from the left on the second row of the color palette.

**10. Click** on **OK**. The Quarterly Sales Report chart will appear. Your chart is now color coordinated!

## SAVING THE 3-D BAR CHART

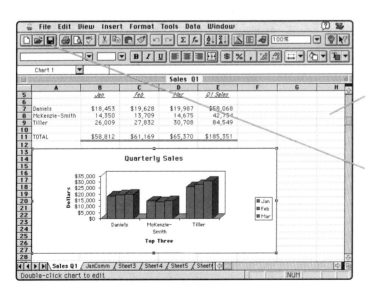

Now that your chart looks like a work of art, you will want to save it.

**1. Click twice anywhere** on the **spreadsheet** to turn off the selection of the graph.

**2. Click** on the **Save button** on the toolbar. Your chart is now saved as part of the Sales Q1 worksheet.

If you plan to follow along to the next chapter, leave the chart on your screen.

# Working with Floors and Walls

You can add a lot of pizzazz to a 3-D chart by decorating the walls and floor. You can not only color the walls and floor in a chart, but you can also add gridlines to the wall to make it easier to line up the columns with the numbers they represent. In this chapter, you will do the following:

❖ Change the floor color of the chart
❖ Change the wall color of the chart
❖ Add horizontal gridlines using the Chart toolbar

## CHANGING THE FLOOR COLOR

1. **Open** the **SALESQ1 worksheet** if it is not already on your screen.

2. **Click twice** on the white space on the **chart** to select it. The border of the chart will become a striped pattern.

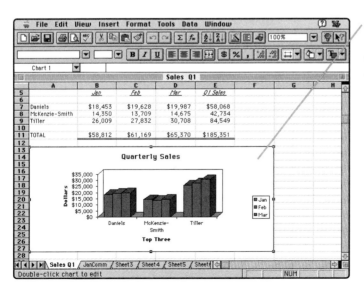

3. **Click twice anywhere** on the **floor** of the chart (the gray, shaded area). The Format Floor dialog box will appear.

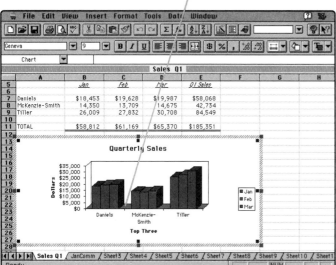

4. **Click** on the **magenta square**, the second from the right in the top row of the palette. Notice that the color will appear in the Sample box.

5. **Click** on **OK**. The Quarterly Sales Report chart will reappear.

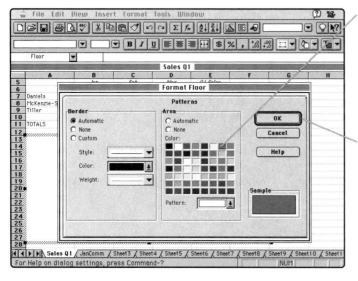

# CHANGING THE WALL COLOR

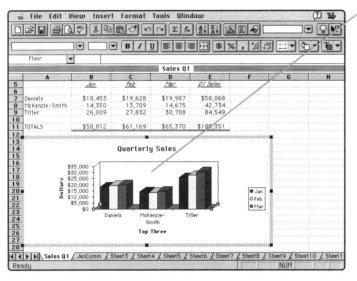

1. **Click twice anywhere** on the **back wall** of the SALESQ1 chart. The Format Walls dialog box will appear.

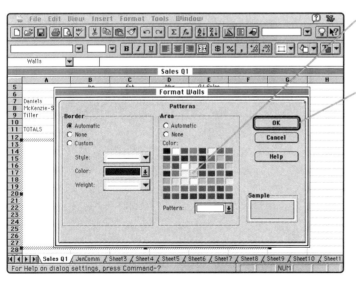

2. **Click** on the **blue square**, the fourth from the left in the fourth row.

3. **Click** on **OK**. The Quarterly Sales Report chart will reappear with a new color added to the chart.

# ADDING GRIDLINES
# WITH THE CHART TOOLBAR

The easiest way to add gridlines to a chart is to use the Chart toolbar, which you closed in Chapter 17, to improve the view. In this section, you will open the chart toolbar and add gridlines.

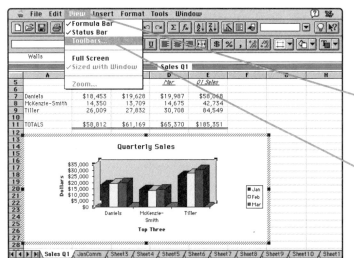

**1. Press and hold** on **View** in the menu bar. A pull-down menu will appear.

**2. Drag** the highlight bar to **Toolbars**, then **release** the mouse button. The Toolbars dialog box will appear.

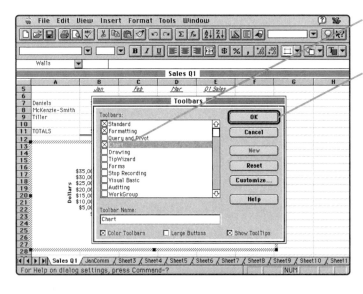

**3. Click** on **Chart** to place an X in the Box.

**4. Click** on **OK**. The Quarterly Sales Report chart will reappear with the chart toolbar.

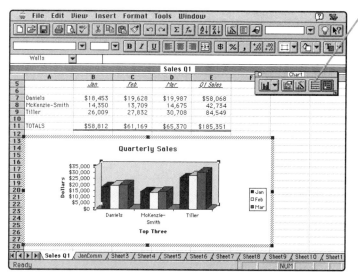

5. **Click** on the **Horizontal Gridlines button** on the toolbar. Gridlines will be added to the walls of the chart.

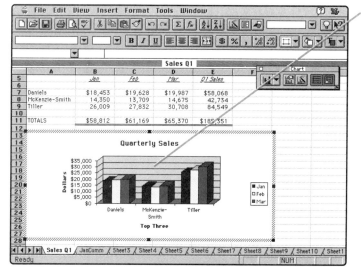

Now notice how much easier it is to read the chart with gridlines.

# SAVING THE CHART

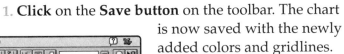

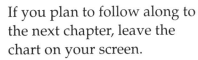

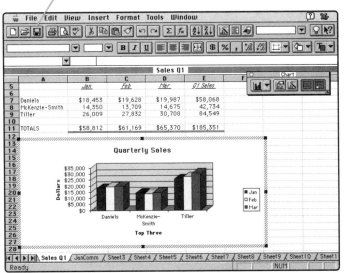

1. **Click** on the **Save button** on the toolbar. The chart is now saved with the newly added colors and gridlines.

If you plan to follow along to the next chapter, leave the chart on your screen.

# Working with Legends and Axis Text

A legend on a map tells you what the symbols on the map mean. Similarly, a chart legend tells you the meaning of the various colors (or shades of gray) of the chart columns. Axis text is the label on either the X or Y axis. The horizontal axis (X axis) text in the example lists the salespeople's names. The vertical axis (Y axis) shows the amount of sales in dollars. In this chapter, you will do the following:

❖ Change the Y-axis text alignment
❖ Change the Y-axis text
❖ Change the legend format
❖ Delete and restore a legend
❖ Move a legend
❖ Close the chart toolbar

## CHANGING THE Y-AXIS TEXT ALIGNMENT

In this section, you will change the alignment of the Y-axis text to horizontal.

1. **Open** the **Sales Q1 worksheet** if it is not already on your screen.

2. **Click twice** on the white area of the **chart** to select the chart, if it isn't already selected. The border will be surrounded by a striped pattern.

3. **Click** once on **Dollars**. Dollars will be surrounded by a box with small, black handles to indicate that it has been selected.

**4. Press and hold** on **Format** in the menu bar. A pull-down menu will appear.

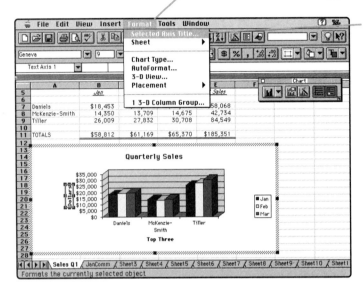

5. **Drag** the highlight bar to **Selected Axis Title**, and **release** the mouse button. The Format Axis Title dialog box will appear.

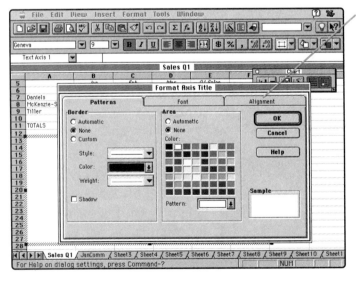

6. **Click** on **Alignment**. The Alignment tab dialog box will appear.

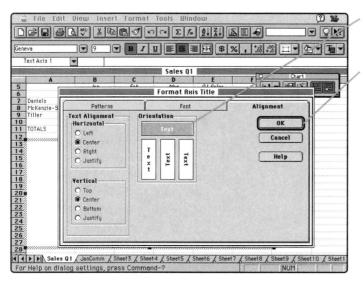

7. **Click** on **Text** (the horizontal box).

8. **Click** on **OK**. The Quarterly Sales Report chart will appear.

Notice that the text, "Dollars," is now aligned horizontally.

## CHANGING THE Y-AXIS TEXT

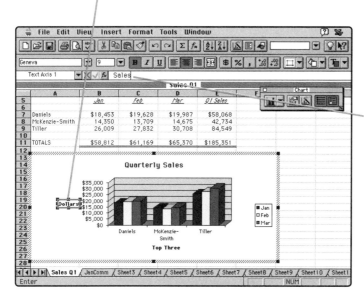

In this section, you will replace the Y-axis text "Dollars" with the text "Sales."

1. **Move** the **mouse pointer** up to the **contents box**. The pointer will change to an I-beam.

2. **Click once** to set the cursor and **type Sales**.

3. **Click** on **✔ or press Return**. The Quarterly Sales Report chart will reappear.

Notice that the text "Dollars" has been replaced by the text "Sales."

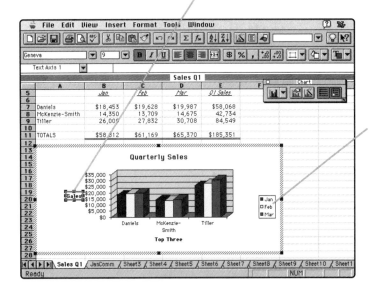

# CHANGING THE LEGEND FORMAT

1. **Click twice anywhere** on the **Legend box**. The legend box will be surrounded with small, black handles. The Format legend dialog box appears.

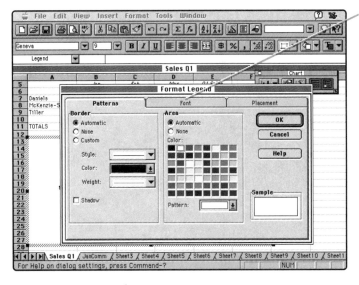

2. **Click** on the **Font tab**. The Font dialog box will appear.

Notice that you can view the list of fonts that are available by clicking on the ⬇ on the scroll bar.

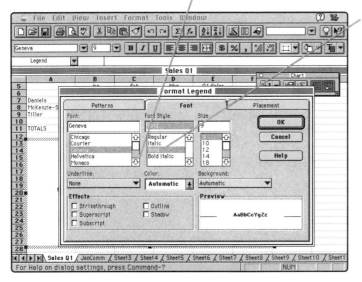

**3. Click** on **Bold** to change the font style. Bold will appear in the Font Style box.

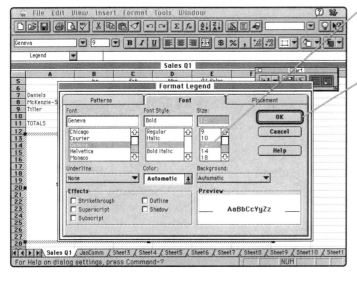

**4. Click** on **12** to change the point size. Twelve (12) will appear in the Size text box.

**5. Click** on **OK**. The Quarterly Sales Report chart will appear. The legend text will now be 12-point Geneva Bold.

# DELETING AND RESTORING A LEGEND

To delete and restore a legend, it is not necessary to have the legend selected.

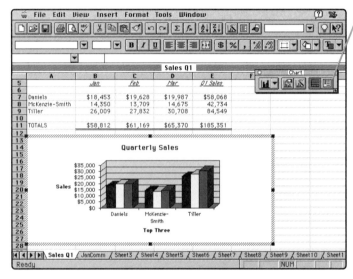

1. **Click** on the **Legend button** on the Chart toolbar. The legend will be deleted.

2. **Click again** on the **Legend button** on the toolbar. The legend will be restored to the chart.

Notice that when the legend is restored, it does not retain the 12-point bold formatting created previously in "Changing the Legend Format."

# MOVING A LEGEND

In this section, you will move the legend to the lower left corner of the chart.

1. **Click** on the **legend** if it does not alredy have selection handles.

2. **Press and hold** the mouse button as you **drag** down to the **bottom** of the **chart**. A dotted frame will move as you drag.

3. **Continue holding** the mouse button and **drag** the dotted **frame** to the **left corner** of the chart.

4. **Release** the **mouse button** when the dotted frame for the legend is placed in the left corner of the chart. The legend text will move to the left corner.

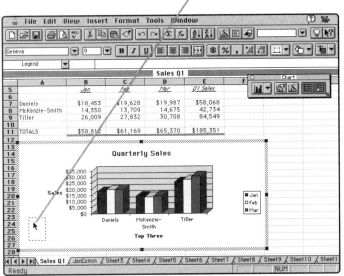

## CLOSING THE CHART TOOLBAR

Notice that the legend appears in the exact location where you placed the dotted frame.

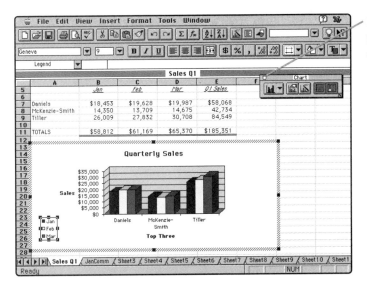

1. **Click once** on the **Close box** on the Chart toolbar. The toolbar will close.

# SAVING THE CHART

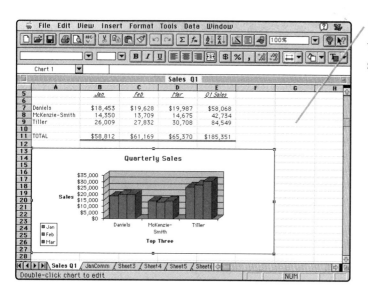

1. **Click anywhere** on the **worksheet** to remove the striped border.

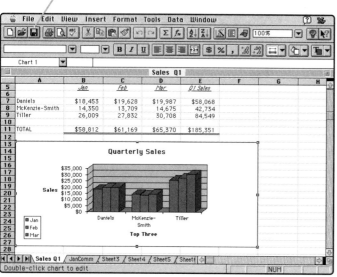

2. **Click** on the **Save button** on the toolbar. The Quarterly Sales Report chart and the worksheet are now saved with the new formatting.

If you plan to follow along with the next chapter, leave the chart on your screen.

# Adding Chart Text, Shapes, and Arrows

Customizing a chart in Excel 5 is a snap. As you saw in the examples in the previous chapter, you can move a chart text box anywhere on the chart by simply clicking on the text box and dragging it to another location. You also saw that you can style text and change text alignment with the Format menu. As you will see in this chapter, you can add additional text boxes (in addition to those automatically created by Excel) and put them anywhere on the chart. Moreover, you can draw arrows and other shapes and place them anywhere on the chart. In this chapter, you will do the following:

❖ Add text to the chart and draw an oval around the text
❖ Color an oval
❖ Add an arrow

## ADDING TEXT

1. **Open** the **Sales Q1** worksheet if it isn't already on your screen.

2. **Click twice** on the **chart**. It will be surrounded by a striped border.

3. **Type Number 1!** (Be sure to include the exclamation point.) As you begin to type, the letters will show up in the formula bar. The Cancel box (X) and the Enter box (✔) will appear.

4. **Click** on ✔ or **press Return**. The text will appear on the chart surrounded by black handles.

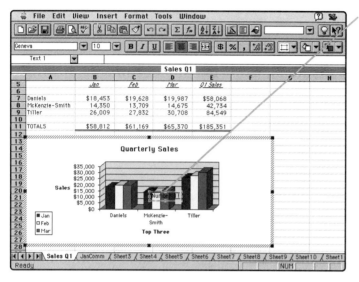

Notice that the text box mysteriously placed itself in this location. Your text box may end up in a different place. The next step is to move it to a different location.

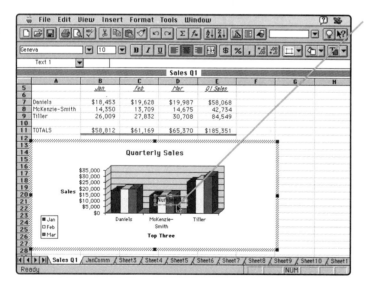

5. **Place** the **mouse pointer** on the **border** of the text box. Do not place it on one of the handles.

6. **Press and hold** the mouse button. When you begin to drag in the next step, a dotted box will appear.

7. While pressing and holding the mouse button, **drag** the **dotted box** to a place on the chart where you want the "Number 1!" text to appear. The "Number 1!" text will not move until you release the mouse button. **Note:** In the next section, you will draw an oval around the text. In the section following it, you will draw an arrow from the text to Tiller's highest column. Place the text so that there is room for the oval and arrow.

8. **Release** the mouse button. The text will move to the new location.

9. **Click** on **any blank spot** on the **chart**. The border will disappear from the text box.

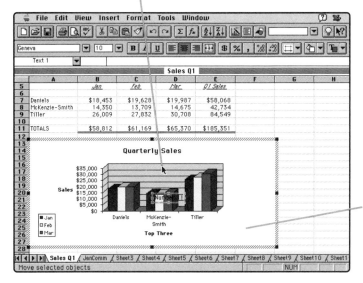

## DRAWING AN OVAL AROUND THE TEXT

In this section, you will draw an oval around the text, "Number 1!"

1. **Click** on the **Drawing button** on the toolbar. The Drawing toolbar will appear as you see in this example.

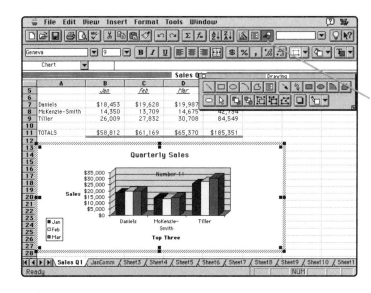

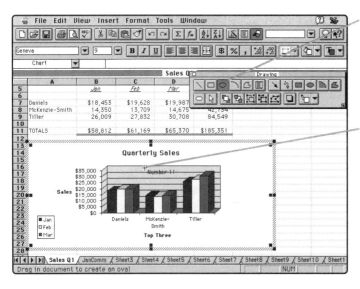

2. **Click** on the **oval button** on the Drawing toolbar. The button will become recessed. The cursor will become a crosshair.

3. **Move** the **crosshair** to the **left** of the **text** where you want to begin drawing the oval (ellipse).

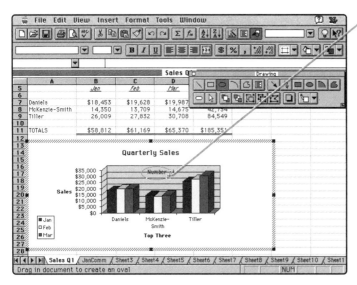

4. **Press and hold** the mouse button as you **drag** the **crosshair down** and to the **right**.

Notice that an oval will form as you drag the crosshair. The idea is to surround "Number 1!" with the oval.

5. **Release** the mouse button. The text will be surrounded by an oval. The oval itself will be surrounded by square handles.

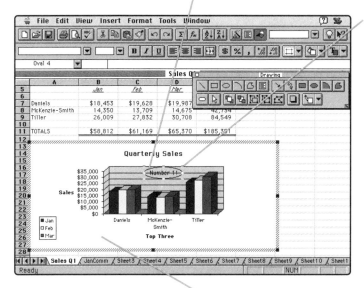

To change the size and shape of the oval, put your mouse pointer on any handle. The pointer will change to a two-headed arrow. **Press and hold** the mouse button as you **drag** the **handle**. Drag toward the middle of the oval to make the oval smaller. Drag out to make it larger. You may have to fiddle with it to get it to look the way you want.

6. **Click once anywhere** on a white area of the **chart**. The black handles will disappear. "Number 1!" will be surrounded by an oval.

## ADDING AN ARROW

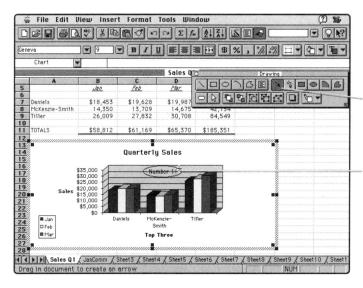

1. **Click** on the **Arrow button**. The cursor will turn into a black crosshair.

2. **Place** the **crosshair** on the **right edge** of the **oval**.

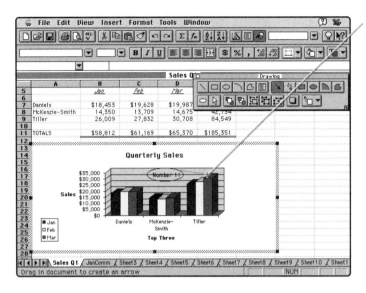

3. **Press and hold** the mouse button as you **drag** the **crosshair** toward the **highest column** in the Tiller area. The arrow line that appears as you drag will look jagged. It will print straight, though.

4. **Release** the mouse button. An arrowhead will be added to the arrow line.

## COLORING THE OVAL

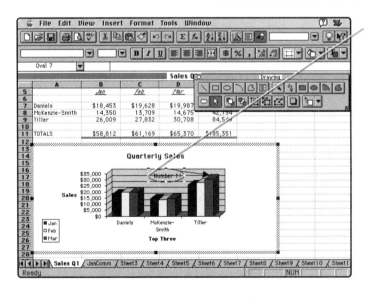

1. **Click** on the **edge** of the **oval**. (You have to be very precise about where you place the mouse arrow before you click or else you may click on the text box by accident). The oval will be surrounded by square handles.

**2. Press and hold** on **Format** in the menu bar. A pull-down menu will appear.

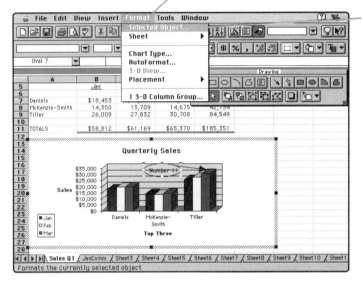

**3. Drag** the highlight bar to **Selected Object**, then **release** the mouse button. The Format Object dialog box will appear.

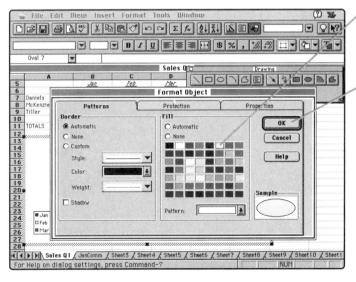

**4. Click** on the **yellow square**, the third from the right in the top row.

**5. Click** on **OK**. The chart will reappear with a yellow background in the oval.

# ARRANGING OBJECTS

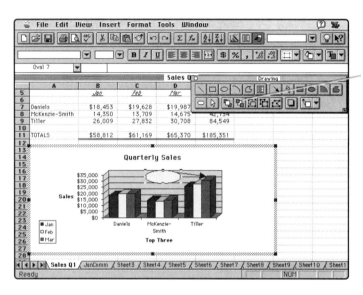

Notice that the yellow oval covers the text.

1. While the oval is selected, **click** on the **Send to Back button** on the Drawing toolbar. The color will go to the background and the text will show.

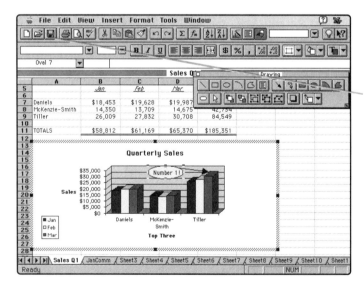

# SAVING THE CHART

1. **Click** on the **Save button**.

Isn't this great? You now have a terrific-looking 3-D column chart. If you want to get even more sophisticated, complete the next two chapters!

# Grouping and Moving Graphics

If you've worked with graphics and text boxes before, you know how frustrating it can be to move them around one at a time when you want to place them somewhere else on your chart. Excel 5 makes this an easy task by allowing you to group several objects together and move them as a unit. In this chapter, you will do the following:

❖ Group together an oval, text box, and arrow
❖ Move the group to a new location
❖ Close the drawing toolbar
❖ Save the chart

## GROUPING AN OVAL, TEXT BOX, AND ARROW

In this section, you will make several graphic elements into a group by drawing a "lasso" around them.

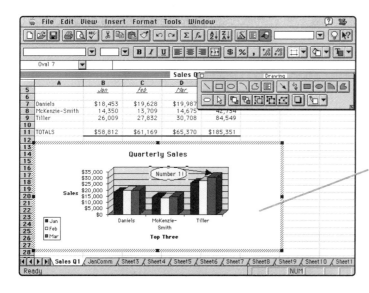

1. **Open** the **Drawing toolbar** if it is not already open. If you need help opening the Drawing toolbar, see page 161, the section entitled "Drawing an Oval Around the Text."

2. **Click twice** in the white area of the **chart**. It will be surrounded by a striped border.

3. **Click** on the **white arrow** on the Drawing toolbar. It will become recessed.

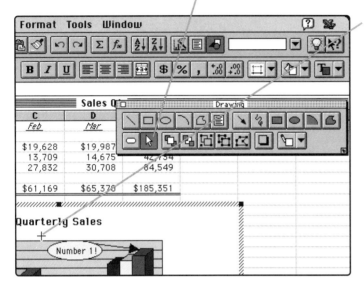

4. **Place** the **mouse arrow** above and to the left of the **oval**. When you press the mouse button, the arrow will become a crosshair.

5. **Press and hold** the mouse button as you **drag** the crosshair **down** and to the **right**. Make sure you get the entire arrow inside the lasso. The oval, the text box, and the arrow will become surrounded by a dotted, rectangular frame.

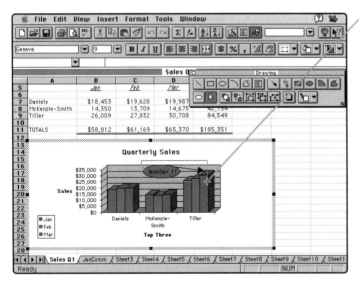

6. **Release** the mouse button. The oval, text box, and arrow are now "grouped together" and all are surrounded by handles. If all of the elements are not surrounded by handles, it means you did not place the crosshair far enough outside the oval. If this happens, click anywhere in the white area of the chart. This will remove the lasso. Repeat steps 3 through 6 to create another lasso.

# MOVING THE GROUPED TEXT AND GRAPHICS

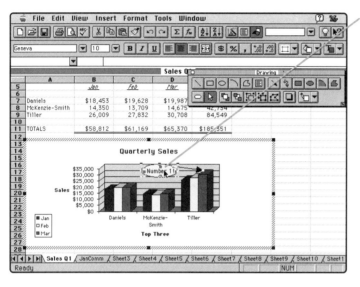

1. **Place** the **mouse arrow** anywhere on the **oval**.

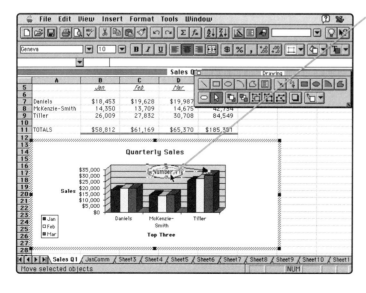

2. **Press and hold** the mouse button as you **move** the **group** to another location to better line it up. You may have to fiddle with this to improve the "look."

3. **Click** once **anywhere** on the worksheet to remove the border.

# CLOSING THE DRAWING TOOLBAR

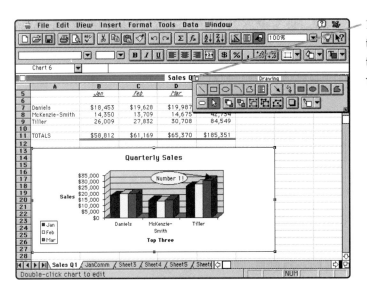

1. **Click** on the **Close box** on the left side of the Drawing title bar. The drawing toolbar will disappear.

# SAVING THE CHART

1. **Click** on the **Save button**.

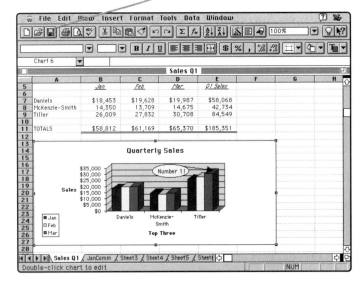

If you plan to follow along to the next chapter, leave the chart on the screen.

# Styling a Chart

In Excel, there are many ways you can make your chart more attractive. You can change the text fonts, background color, and patterns and even add colored borders around text blocks. You are limited only by your imagination! If you are printing in black and white, the Patterns option improves a chart's appearance when you print. In this chapter, you will do the following:

❖ Add a colored border and shadow to a text box
❖ Change the font in a text box
❖ Add a colored border around the chart area
❖ Add and remove patterns on the columns

## ADDING A COLORED BORDER AND SHADOW

In this section, you will add a colored border with a shadow to the chart title text box.

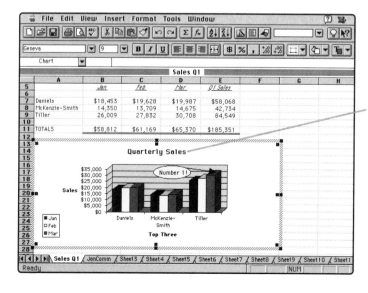

1. **Click twice anywhere** on the **chart** if it is not surrounded by a striped border.

2. **Click twice** on the chart title, **Quarterly Sales**. The Format Chart Title dialog box will appear. If it doesn't, click on several different items on the chart and then click off the chart and start again.

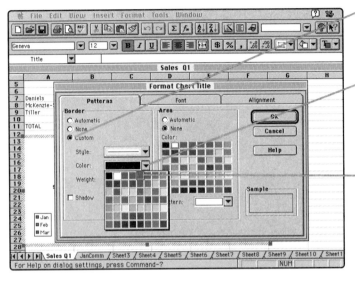

3. **Click** on **Custom** in the Border image area to place a dot in the circle.

4. **Press and hold** on the ▼ to the right of color. A drop-down Color palette will appear.

5. **Drag** the highlight bar to the **blue square** in the top row, the fifth square from the left. **Release** the mouse button. The blue color will appear in the sample color box.

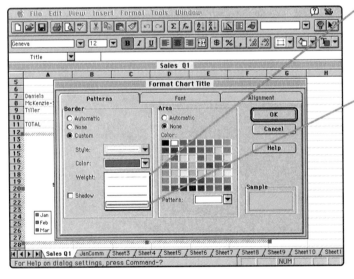

6. **Press and hold** on the ▼ to the right of the Weight box. A drop-down list of border options will appear.

7. **Drag** the mouse pointer to the **border option** shown here. **Release** the mouse button. It will appear in the Weight box, and the sample border will show in the Sample box.

8. **Click** on **Shadow** to put an ✕ in the box. The Sample box will now show the shadow.

9. **Click** on **OK**. The Quarterly Sales chart will reappear.

10. **Click anywhere** on the **white section** of the chart. The selection handles will disappear.

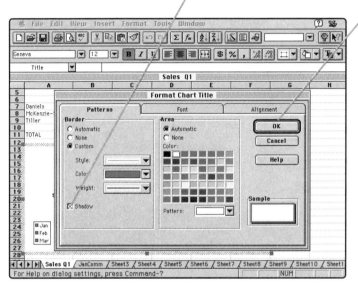

## CHANGING THE FONT IN A TEXT BOX

In this example, you will change the font in the Number 1 text box to bold.

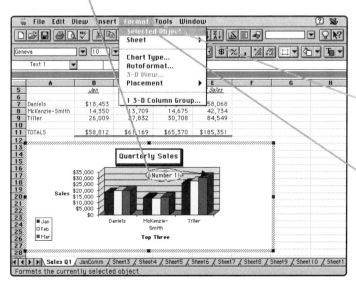

1. **Click** on **Number 1!** The text box will be surrounded by a border with handles.

2. **Press and hold** on **Format** in the menu bar. A pull-down menu will appear.

3. **Drag** the highlight bar to **Selected Object**, then **release** the mouse button. The Format Object dialog box will appear.

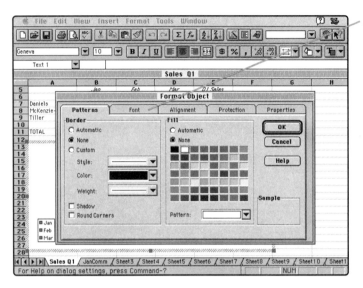

4. **Click** on the **Font tab**. The Font Format dialog box will appear.

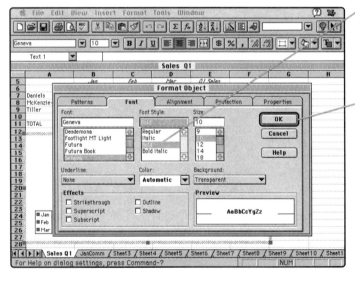

5. **Click** on **Bold**. Bold will become highlighted and the word Bold will appear in the font style box.

6. **Click** on **OK**. The chart will appear.

7. **Click anywhere** on the **white surface** of the chart. The selection handles will disappear.

# ADDING A BORDER
# TO A CHART

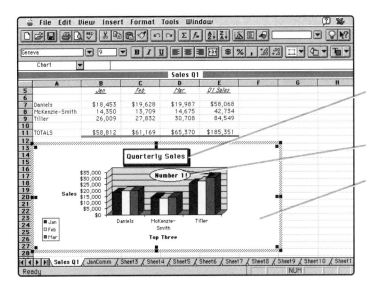

In this section, you will add a red border to surround the chart area.

Notice the blue border and shadow.

Notice the bold font.

**1.** **Click anywhere** on the **white surface** of the chart. Handles will appear just inside the striped border.

**2.** **Press and hold** on **Format** in the menu bar. A pull-down menu will appear.

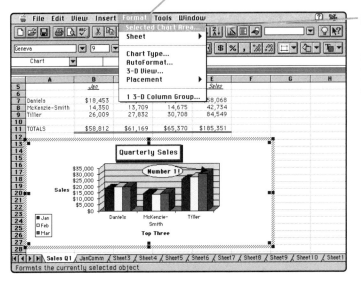

**3.** **Drag** the highlight bar to **Selected Chart Area**, then **release** the mouse button. The Format Chart Area dialog box will appear.

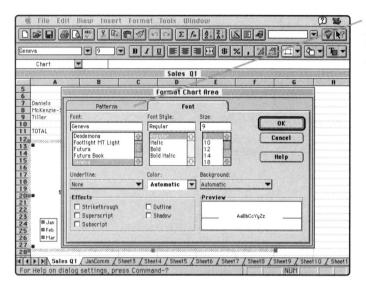

4. **Click** on **Patterns**. The Patterns dialog box will appear.

5. **Click** on **Custom** to place a dot in the circle.

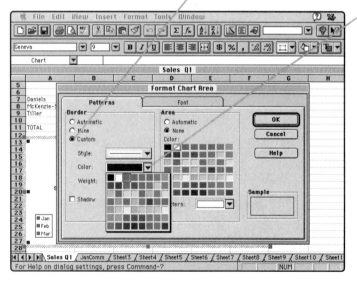

6. **Press and hold** on the ▼ in the color text box. A drop-down color palette will appear.

7. **Drag** the mouse pointer to the **red square**, the third square from the left in the top row. Release the mouse button. The red square will appear in the sample color box.

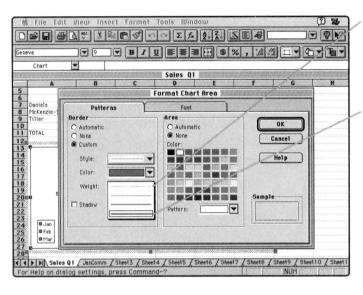

8. **Press and hold** on the ▼ to the right of the Weight box. A drop-down list of border weights will appear.

9. **Drag** the mouse pointer to the **border** at the bottom of the list. Release the mouse button. It will appear in the Weight box.

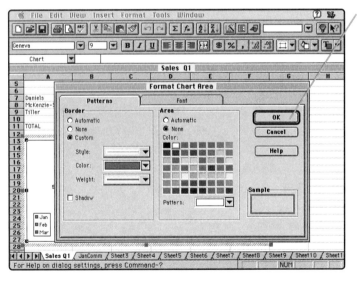

10. **Click** on **OK**. The chart will appear surrounded by a red border.

# ADDING A PATTERN
# TO A CHART COLUMN

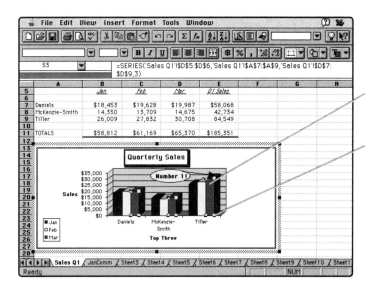

In this section, you will add a pattern to the March column for the three sales executives.

1. **Click** on **Tiller's March column**.

Notice that the white handles appear on the March columns of the three salespeople.

2. **Press and hold** on **Format** in the menu bar. A pull-down menu will appear.

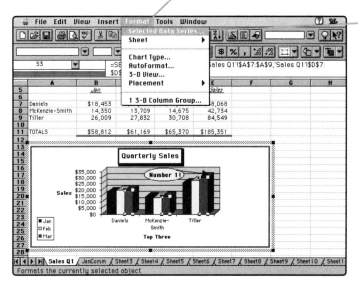

3. **Drag** the highlight bar to **Selected Series**, then **release** the mouse button. The Format Data Series dialog box will appear.

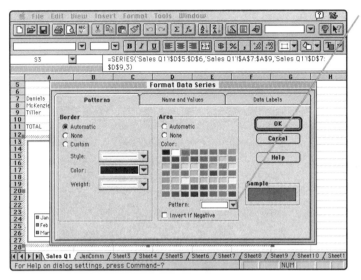

4. **Press and hold** on the ▼ to the right of Pattern. A pop-up pattern palette will appear.

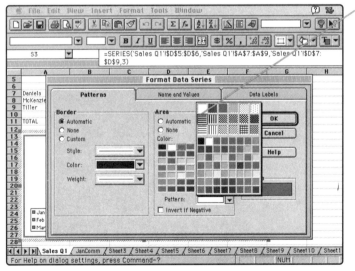

5. **Drag** the mouse pointer to the **first pattern** in the second row from the top. Release the mouse button. The pattern will appear in the Sample box.

Notice the pattern in the Sample box.

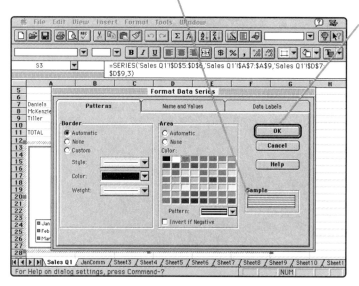

6. **Click** on **OK**. The chart will reappear with the striped pattern you selected for the March columns.

Note: You can repeat steps 1 through 6 to put different patterns on the Jan and Feb columns.

## REMOVING THE PATTERNS

Make certain that the columns from which you want to remove the patterns are selected.

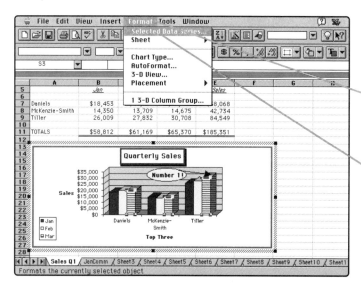

Note: The March columns should be selected with white handles.

1. **Press and hold** on **Format** on the menu bar. A pull-down menu will appear.

2. **Drag** the highlight bar to **Selected Data Series**, then **release** the mouse button. The Format Data Series dialog box will appear.

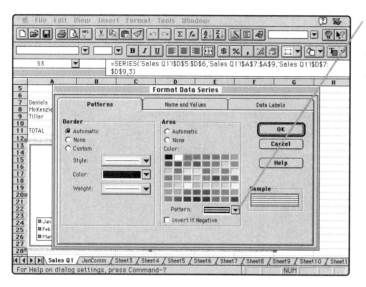

3. **Press and hold** on the ▼ to the right of the Pattern text box. A pop-up pattern palette will appear.

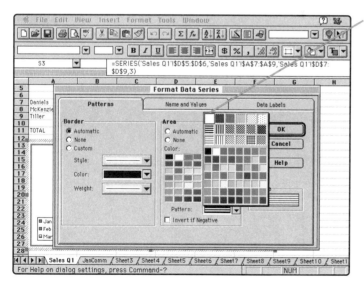

4. **Drag** the mouse pointer to the **white square** in the top left corner of the pattern palette. Release the mouse button. The pop-up palette will disappear. The Pattern box will be white, and the Sample box will be solid red.

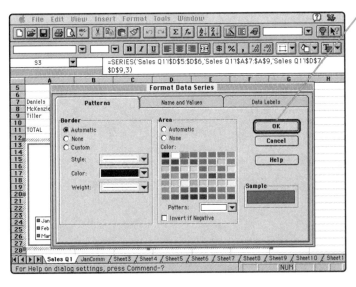

5. **Click** on **OK**. Voilà! The columns are now solid red!

6. **Click twice** off the chart area. The chart will be surrounded by the red border. The selection handles and striped border will disappear.

## SAVING THE STYLE

1. **Click** on the **Save button** on the toolbar.

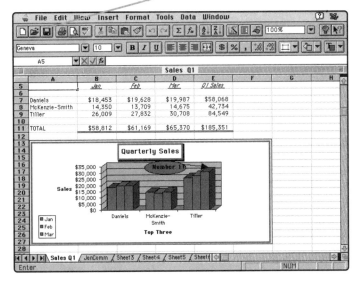

If you plan to follow along to the next chapter, leave the chart on your screen.

# Copying and Printing Charts

In Excel 5, you can put a chart on a different sheet within the workbook file. This makes it easy to print the chart without the worksheet data. The chart remains linked to the original worksheet data, however, so that any changes you make in the worksheet are reflected in the chart. If you leave the chart in the worksheet where you created it, you can print both the chart and worksheet data together. In this chapter, you will do the following:

❖ Copy a chart to a separate sheet within the workbook
❖ Print a chart
❖ Print a chart and a worksheet on the same page
❖ Preview and print a chart and a worksheet sideways (in landscape orientation)

## COPYING THE CHART TO ANOTHER SHEET

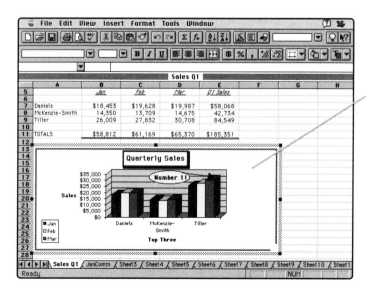

In this section, you will copy a chart to another sheet and save it.

1. **Click twice** on the white area of the **chart**. It will become surrounded by a striped border with handles.

2. **Click** on the **Copy button** in the toolbar. The chart will be surrounded by a border of running ants.

3. **Click** on the **Sheet 3 tab**. An empty worksheet will appear.

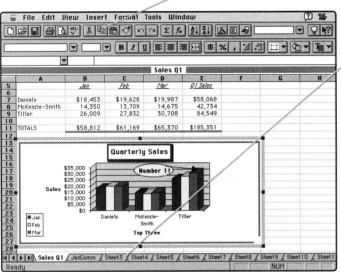

4. **Click** on the **Paste button** on the toolbar. A copy of the chart will appear on the sheet.

Note: When you click on the Paste button, the chart that is copied to the worksheet remains linked to the original embedded chart. When you make a change in the data in the Sales Q1 worksheet, therefore, the changes will be reflected in this chart.

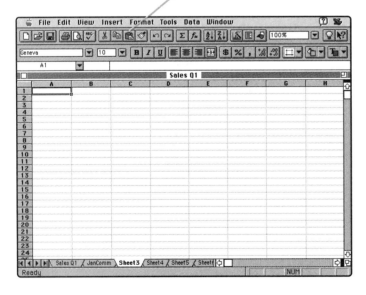

## PRINTING THE CHART

1. **Click** on the **Print button** in the toolbar. A printing message box will appear briefly. After a short intermission, the chart will print.

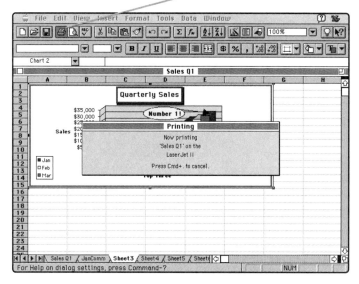

## NAMING AND SAVING THE SHEET

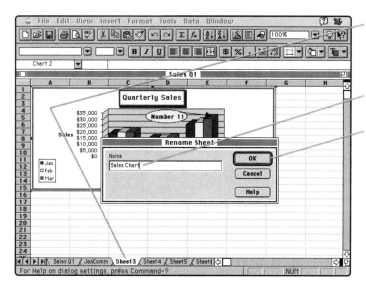

1. **Click twice** on **Sheet3**. The Rename Sheet dialog box will appear.

2. **Type Sales Chart**.

3. **Click** on **OK**. The rename Sheet dialog box will appear.

4. **Click** on the **Save button** on the toolbar. A copy of the Quarterly Sales chart is now saved to a new sheet.

Notice the new name for the tab.

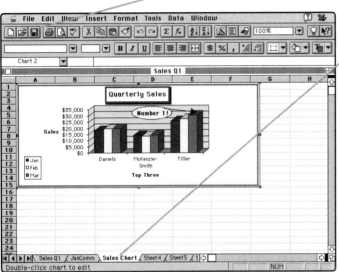

## PRINTING A WORKSHEET AND A CHART AT THE SAME TIME

1. **Click** on the **Sales Q1 tab**. The first worksheet and chart will appear.

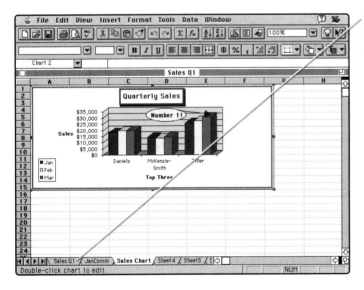

2. **Click** on the **Print button** in the toolbar. The Printing message box will appear. The Sales Q1 worksheet and chart will be printed together on the same page.

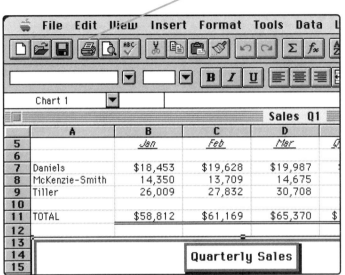

3. If you change your mind, **press and hold** the **Command key** as you press the **. (period) key**.

## PRINTING A WORKSHEET AND CHART SIDEWAYS

There may be a time when you will want to print both a worksheet and a chart sideways (in landscape orientation) on your paper, especially if your worksheet is quite wide.

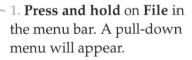

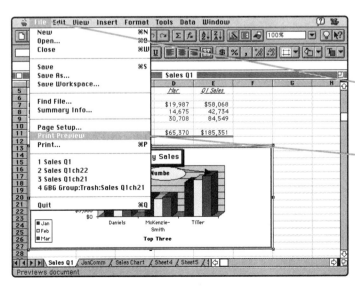

1. **Press and hold** on **File** in the menu bar. A pull-down menu will appear.

2. **Drag** the highlight bar to **Print Preview**. Then **release** the mouse button. The Print Preview screen will appear.

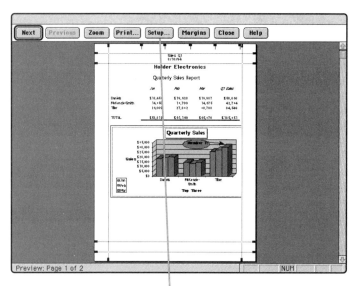

Most documents are normally printed in portrait orientation, with the short side of the paper at the top. This is what you will see the first time you select the Print Preview option. This preview is an example of a portrait orientation.

If you notice that the chart is too big for the page, you'll readjust this in step 5 below.

3. **Click** on **Setup**. The Page Setup dialog box will appear.

Landscape printing means printing with the long side of the paper on top. Landscape printing is often used to print financial worksheets and charts that are too wide to be printed in portrait.

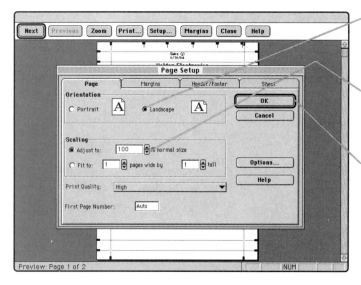

4. **Click** on **Landscape** in the Orientation option box to place a dot inside the circle.

5. **Click repeatedly** on the ▼ to the right of the Adjust to box to change the scale to 100.

6. **Click** on **OK**. The worksheet and chart will appear in landscape orientation in the print preview screen.

6. **Click** on **Print**. The Print Preview screen will disappear. The Print dialog box will appear.

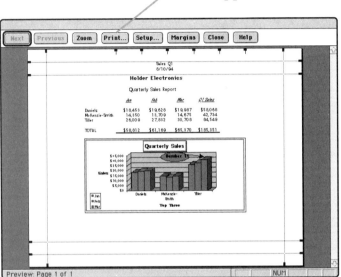

7. **Click** on **Print**. The Printing message box will appear briefly. The worksheet and chart will be printed sideways.

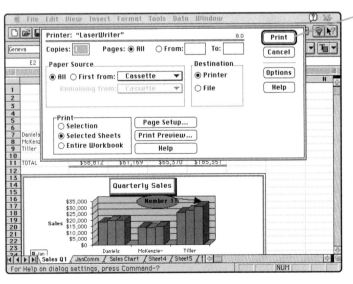

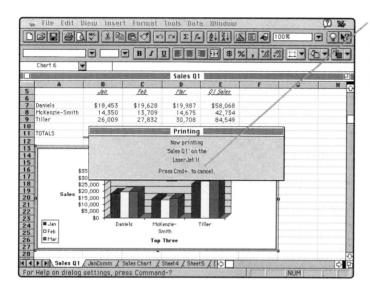

If you want to cancel the printing job, **press and hold** the ⌘ **key** as you **press** the **period (.) key**.

## Switching Back to Portrait Printing

It is a good idea to switch back to portrait printing at this time. Otherwise, the next time you print something it will be printed sideways.

1. **Press and hold** on **File** in the menu bar. A pull-down menu will appear.

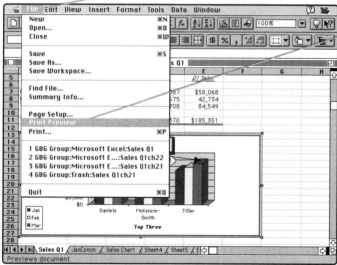

2. **Drag** the highlight bar to **Print Preview**, then **release** the mouse button. The Print Preview screen will appear. The preview window will show the worksheet in landscape orientation.

3. **Click** on **Setup**. The Page Setup dialog box will reappear.

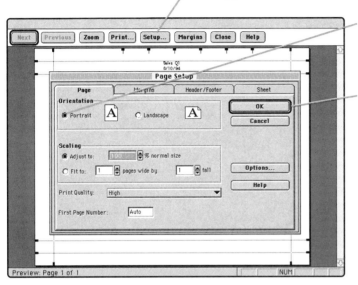

4. **Click** on **Portrait** in the Orientation option box to place a dot inside the circle.

5. **Click** on **OK**. The Print Preview screen will show the worksheet in portrait orientation.

Your printer will now print in portrait mode.

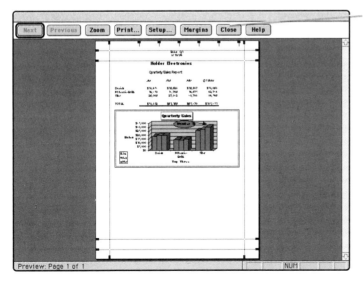

6. **Click** on **Close**. The Quarterly Sales Report chart will appear.

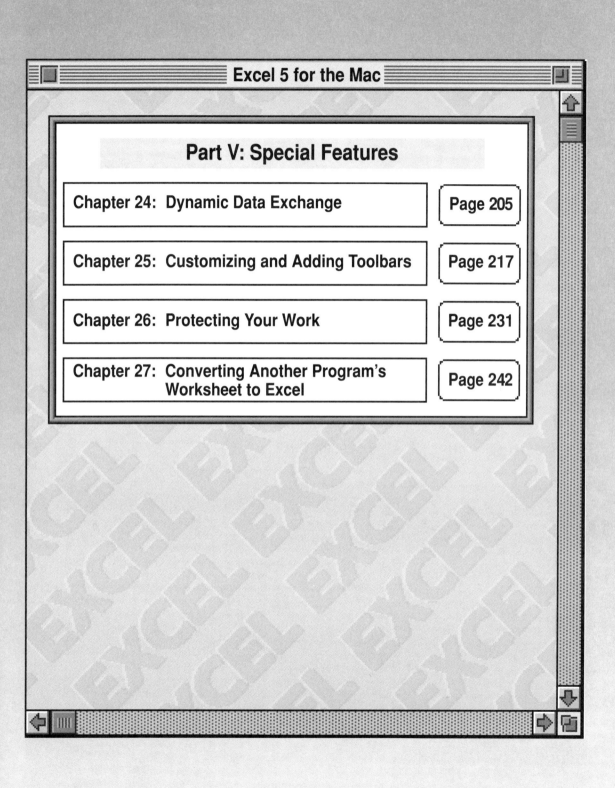

# Excel 5 for the Mac

## Part V: Special Features

# Dynamic
# Data Exchange

Another terrific feature of Excel is that you can link a worksheet chart into a word-processed document. When a worksheet chart is linked to a word-processed document, *any changes made in the worksheet chart are automatically reflected* in the document. This feature is called *Dynamic Data Exchange*. In this chapter, you will do the following:

❖ Copy a chart to the Clipboard
❖ Open a Word document file
❖ Paste-link a chart to a Word document
❖ Observe the link in action

## THE COPY-AND-LINK PROCESS

The copy-and-link process described in this chapter consists of four stages:

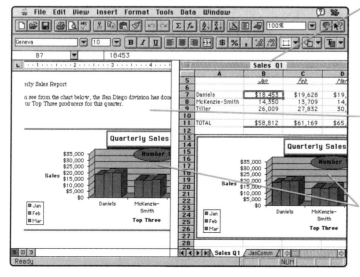

Stage 1: Copy the Excel chart to the Clipboard

Stage 2: Keep Excel running in the background

Stage 3: Open a word-processed document into which you will paste-link the chart

Stage 4: Paste-link a copy of the Excel chart from the clipboard into the word-processed document

# Copying a Chart to the Clipboard

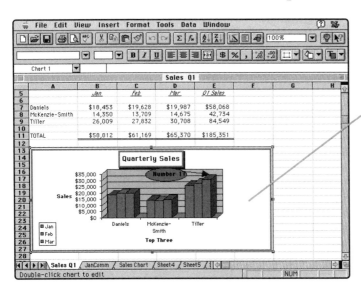

1. **Open** the **Sales Q1** worksheet containing the Quarterly Sales Report you created in Part IV.

2. **Click** in the white area of the **chart** to select it. The chart will be surrounded by a border with handles. Make sure that the striped border is not selected. If it is, click once anywhere on the worksheet and try again.

3. **Press and hold** on **Edit** in the menu bar. A pull-down menu will appear.

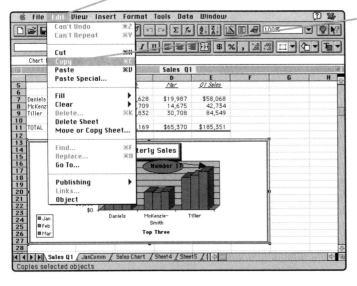

4. **Drag** the highlight bar to **Copy**, then **release** the mouse button. The chart will be copied to the Clipboard. The chart is now ready to be linked to a word-processed document file.

# Running Excel in the Background

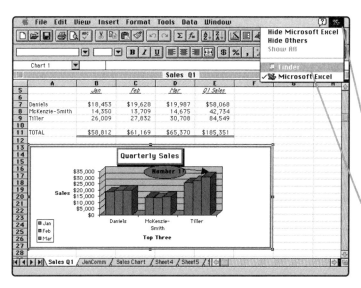

To link the Quarterly Sales Report chart to a word-processed document, Excel must be running.

**1. Press and hold** on the **Excel icon** in the upper right corner of the screen. A pull-down menu will appear.

**2. Drag** the **highlight bar** to **Finder**, then **release** the mouse button. The Excel program window will move to the background.

You may have to navigate your way to the window where your word processing program is. In this example, click on the GBGroup window to make that window active.

# Opening a Word-Processed Document

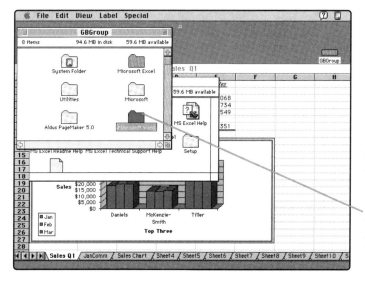

We used Word 6 as the word-processing program in this example. However, other programs link documents in much the same way.

**1. Click twice** on the **folder** of the word-processing program you want to use.

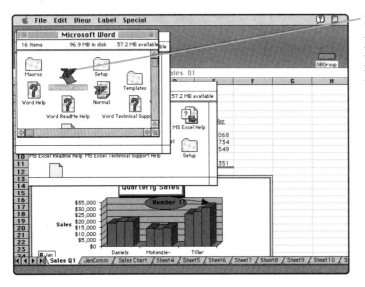

2. **Click twice** on the word-processing icon to open the program. In this example, it is Microsoft Word.

## Linking the Chart

This example shows a maximized screen with the chart being linked to a memo. However, you can link into a blank document if you don't want to bother typing the memo text.

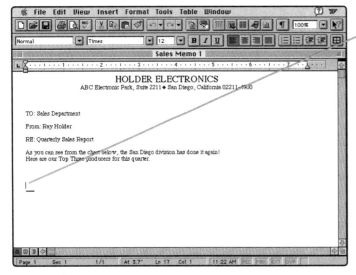

1. **Click** the cursor on the spot where you want to paste-link the copy of the Quarterly Sales chart.

2. **Press and hold** on **Edit** in the menu bar. A pull-down menu will appear.

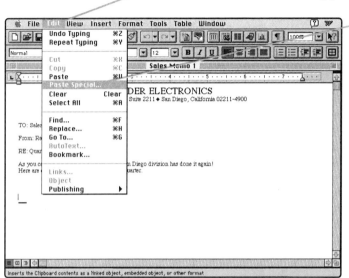

3. **Drag** the **highlight bar** to **Paste Special**, then **release** the mouse button. The Paste Special dialog box will appear.

4. **Click** on **Picture** in the Data Type dialog box. (We recommend that you choose Picture because the file size is smaller and takes up less space on your drive than if you choose Microsoft Excel 5.0 Chart Type.)

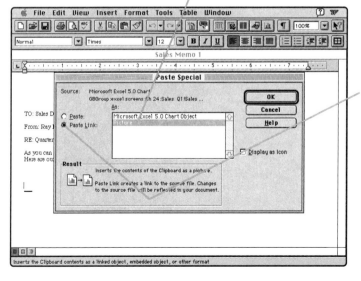

5. **Click** on **Paste Link** to place a dot in the circle.

6. **Click** on **OK**. The Quarterly Sales chart will appear in the word-processed document.

# CENTERING THE CHART IN THE WORD-PROCESSED DOCUMENT

1. **Click** on the **chart** to select it.

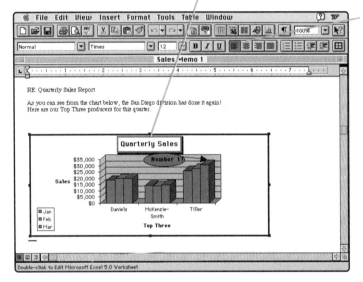

2. **Click** on the **Center button** in the toolbar.

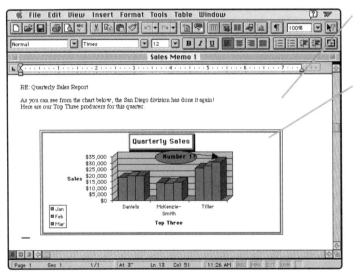

3. **Click once anywhere** on the memo. The chart will no longer appear highlighted.

Notice that the chart is now centered in the memo.

# VIEWING EXCEL AND WORD SIDE BY SIDE

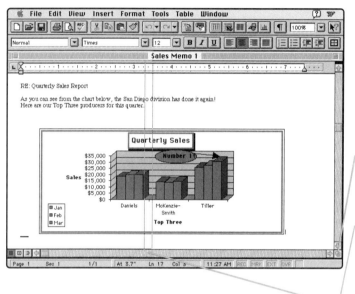

To really appreciate how a link works, you must see it in action. In this section, you will place the Excel worksheet and the word-processed memo side by side (called tiling or layering).

1. **Press and hold** on the **Size box** on the bottom of the window.

2. **Drag** the outline of the **window border** to the left so that it is half the size of the opening screen.

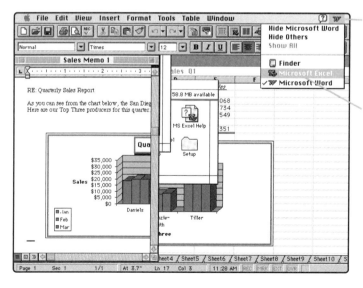

3. **Click** on the **Word Application icon** in the right corner of the menu bar. A pull-down menu will appear.

4. **Drag** the **highlight bar** to **Microsoft Excel**, then **release** the mouse button. The Excel window will appear.

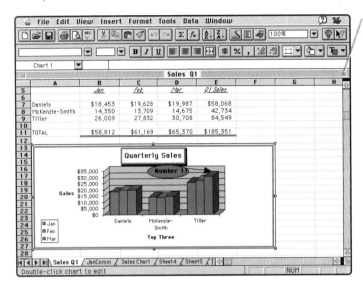

5. **Click** on the **Zoom box** on the right side of the title bar. The Sales Q1 window will shrink.

If the Excel window jumps over on top of the Word window, or otherwise misbehaves, just place the mouse pointer on the title bar, then press, hold and drag the window into position beside the Word window.

Size the Excel window as necessary by repeating steps 1 and 2 on the previous page.

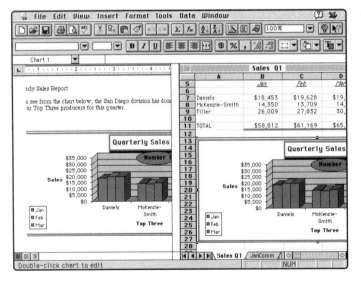

6. **Click repeatedly** on the scroll bars on both windows until your view approximates the one you see in this example. You want to be able to see the Daniels columns on the chart in the word-processing window and, at the same time, see the worksheet sales figures in the Excel window. You may have to fiddle with the two scroll bars in each window to get there.

# TESTING THE LINK

1. **Click anywhere** on the Excel worksheet to make it the active window.

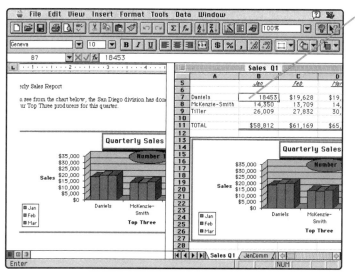

2. **Click twice** on **B7** on the worksheet to open it for in-cell editing. The current sales numbers for this cell will appear in the contents box.

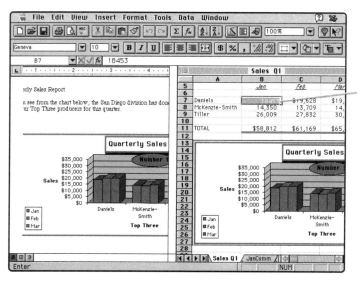

3. **Click twice** in **B7** to highlight the contents of the cell.

4. **Type 60000**.

5. **Press** the **Return key** and watch the fun. Daniels' January column will automatically enlarge in both windows.

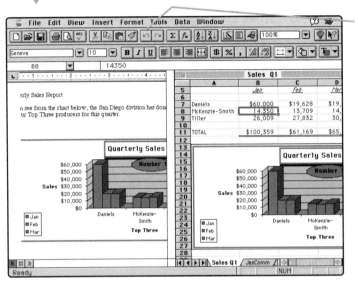

6. **Click** on the **Undo button** in the toolbar to undo the change. The worksheet and the linked chart will return to their original versions.

## Just for Fun!

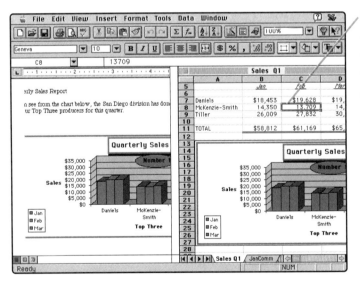

Try changing other numbers on the worksheet and watch the resulting changes in the word-processing document chart.

If you are going to use the Excel worksheet to complete other chapters in this book, remember to change the numbers on the worksheet back to their original amounts.

# CLOSING THE WORD DOCUMENT

1. **Click** in the **Word window** to make it active.

2. **Click** on the **Save button** in the toolbar.

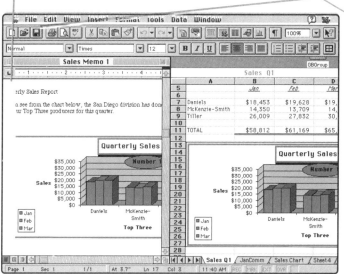

3. **Press and hold** on **File** in the menu bar. A pull-down menu will appear.

4. **Drag** the **highlight bar** to **Quit**, then **release** the mouse button. Word will close.

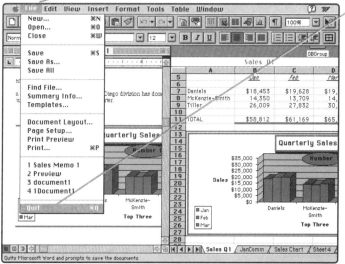

# MAXIMIZING EXCEL

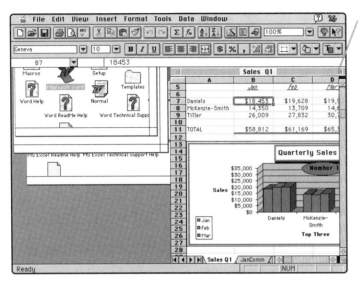

1. **Click** on the **Zoom box** on the right side of the title bar. The Sales Q1 window will expand to fill the screen.

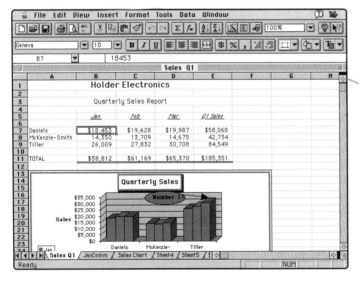

## Changing the View

1. **Click repeatedly** on the ⬆ on the scroll bar to bring the chart into view.

# Customizing and Adding Toolbars

In Excel 5, you can change the look of your workplace by removing or adding toolbars from your screen. You can customize one or more of the standard toolbars or create a new toolbar. You can move buttons around from one toolbar to another and put the buttons you use the most on one toolbar. You can place toolbars in various spots on the screen and make the buttons larger. The layout of your workplace is limited only by your own creativity. In this chapter, you will do the following:

❖ Hide a toolbar
❖ Create a new toolbar
❖ Delete selected toolbar buttons
❖ Move selected toolbar buttons to the new toolbar
❖ Make the toolbar buttons larger
❖ Move a toolbar to a different location
❖ Delete the custom toolbar
❖ Restore the original toolbar

## HIDING A TOOLBAR

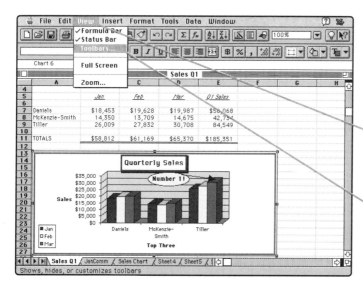

In this section, you will hide the Formatting toolbar.

1. **Open Sales Q1** if it is not already open.

2. **Press and hold** on **View** in the menu bar. A pull-down menu will appear.

3. **Drag** the **highlight bar** to **Toolbars**, then **release** the mouse button. The Toolbars dialog box will appear.

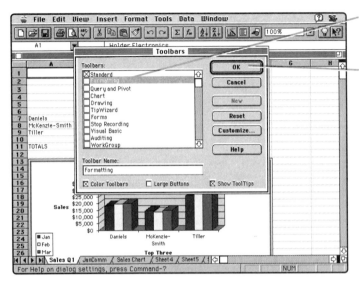

**4. Click** on **Formatting** to *remove* the X from the box.

**5. Click** on **OK**. The Formatting toolbar will no longer appear on the desktop screen.

## CREATING A NEW TOOLBAR

In this section, you will create a new toolbar. In the sections that follow, you will move selected toolbar buttons to the new toolbar.

**1. Place** the **mouse arrow anywhere** on the standard toolbar.

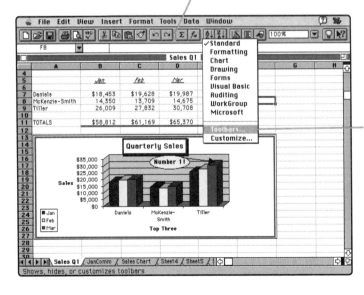

**2. Press and hold** the **Control key**, then **press and hold** the **mouse button**. A pop-up menu will appear. **Release** the **Control** key.

**3. Drag** the **highlight bar** to **Toolbars**, then **release** the mouse button. The Toolbar dialog box will appear.

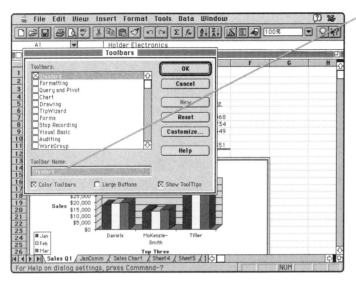

**4. Click twice** on the word "**Standard**" in the Toolbar Name box to highlight it if necessary.

**5. Type My Tools**.

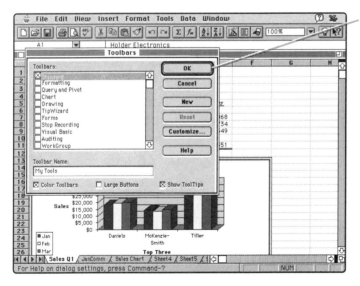

**6. Click** on **OK**. A tiny toolbar will appear in the upper left corner of the screen. The Customize dialog box will appear. You now have an empty toolbar ready to be filled with your favorite tools!

# MOVING A DIALOG BOX

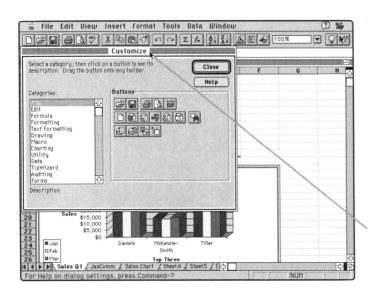

Your dialog box may appear at the top of your screen, as you see in this example. If so, it will not interfere with the steps in the following section, but it will cause your new toolbar to look different from the one you see in these examples. You can move any dialog box very easily.

1. **Place** the mouse arrow on **top** of the dialog box **title bar**.

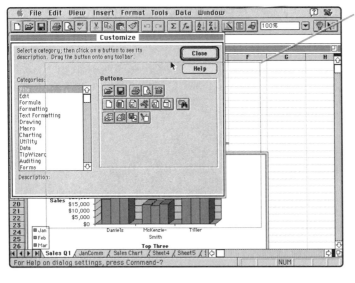

2. **Press and hold** the mouse button and **drag** the dialog box down **toward** the **bottom** of the screen. You will see an outline of the dialog box being dragged.

3. **Release** the mouse button when the outline is positioned where you want the dialog box to be. The dialog box will move into the new position.

# MOVING BUTTONS TO A NEW TOOLBAR

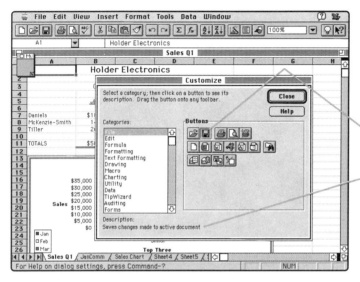

In this section, you will customize the new toolbar with the Save and Print buttons and then add some text formatting buttons.

1. **Click** on the **Save button**. It will become recessed.

Notice that the description of the Save button appears at the bottom of the dialog box.

2. **Click and hold** on the **Save button** and **drag** it to the tiny **toolbar** in the corner. You will see an outline of the button being dragged.

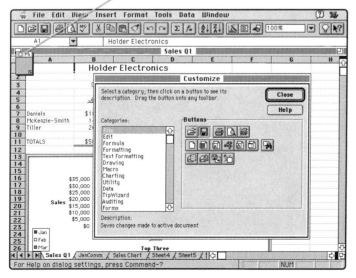

3. **Release** the mouse button. The Save button tool will appear in the new toolbar.

Notice the Save button in the new toolbar.

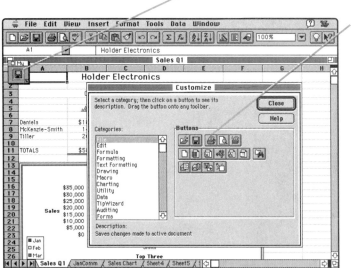

4. **Repeat steps 1 through 3** to place the Print button beside the Save button in the toolbar.

Notice the Print button.

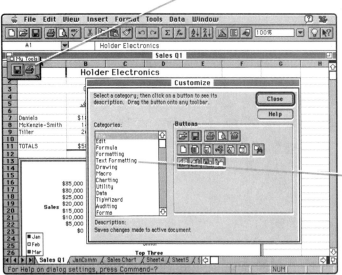

(If, on your screen, the Customize dialog box is to the right of the new My Tools box, the new toolbox will not have room to expand to the right. It will, therefore, expand vertically as you add buttons, instead of horizontally, as you see in this example.)

5. **Click** on **Text Formatting** to highlight it. The text formatting buttons will appear in the buttons box.

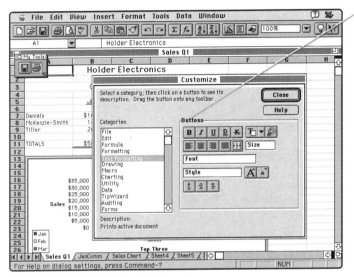

Notice that the selection of button tools has changed.

6. **Repeat steps 1 through 3** to put each of the four alignment buttons from the second row into the new toolbar.

7. **Repeat steps 1 through 3** to place each of the following buttons in the new toolbar:

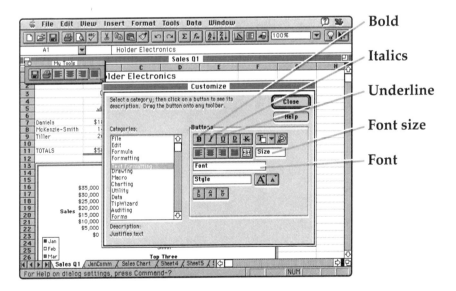

Bold

Italics

Underline

Font size

Font

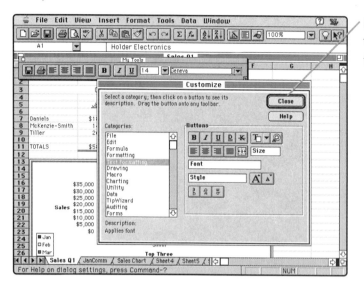

8. **Click** on **Close**. The worksheet will appear with the new toolbar showing.

## MOVING THE NEW TOOLBAR

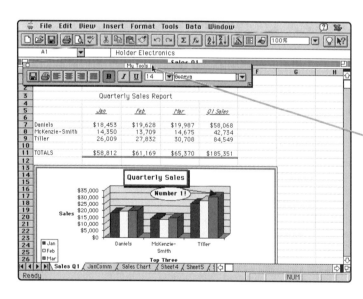

In Excel you can move toolbars to various locations by clicking on the title bar and dragging them. This is called docking.

1. **Place** the **mouse arrow** on the **title bar** of the toolbar.

2. **Press and hold** the mouse button and **drag** up **toward** the **Standard toolbar**. You will drag an outline of the toolbar. The toolbar itself will not move.

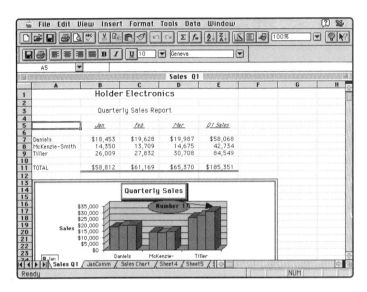

3. **Release** the mouse button when the outline is just below the Standard toolbar. My Tools toolbar will dock itself right under the Standard toolbar. Magic!

## DELETING BUTTONS FROM THE STANDARD TOOLBAR

As you work, you may find that there are buttons you don't use very often. You can delete these to make room for other buttons or to make more space for large buttons. In this section, you will delete buttons from the Standard toolbar that are duplicated on the My Tools toolbar.

1. **Place** the mouse arrow on the **Standard toolbar**.

2. **Press and hold** the **Control key**, then **press and hold** the **mouse button**. A pop-up menu will appear. **Release** the **Control key**.

3. **Drag** the highlight bar to **Customize**, then **release** the mouse button. The Customize dialog box will appear.

4. **Click** on the **Save button** on the Standard toolbar. It will appear to be recessed.

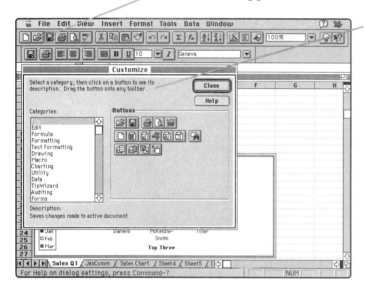

5. **Press and hold** the mouse button as you **drag** the button outline to the **Customize dialog box**.

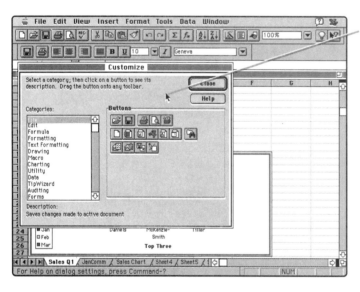

6. **Release** the mouse button anywhere in the dialog box. The Save button will disappear from the Standard toolbar.

Notice that the Save button is gone from the Standard toolbar.

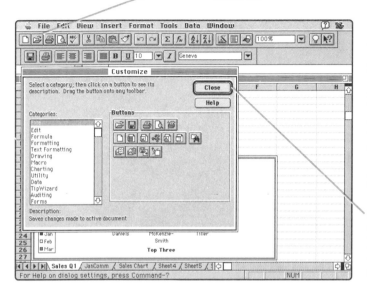

**7.** Repeat steps 5 through 7 to remove each of the following:

**Print button**

**Format Painter button**

**Tip Wizard button**

**Help button**

**8.** **Click** on **Close** when you have finished removing the buttons. The worksheet and chart will reappear.

## MAKING BUTTONS BIGGER

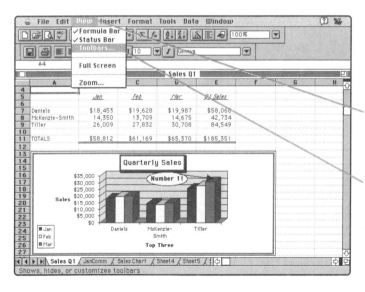

For those of us with bifocals, the ultimate worksheet has larger buttons. Here's how you make buttons larger:

**1.** **Press and hold** on **View** in the menu bar. A pull-down menu will appear.

**2.** **Drag** the highlight bar to **Toolbars**, then **release** the mouse button. The Toolbars dialog box will appear.

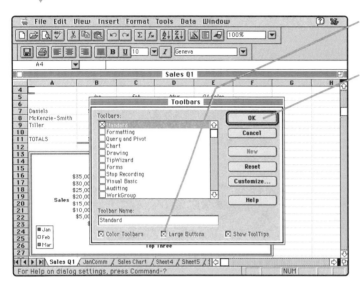

3. **Click** on **Large Buttons** to put an ✕ in the box.

4. **Click** on **OK**. The worksheet and chart will reappear with buttons you can actually see! Wow!

# DELETING THE CUSTOM TOOLBAR

1. **Press and hold** on **View** in the menu bar. A pull-down menu will appear.

2. **Drag** the highlight bar to **Toolbars**, then **release** the mouse button. The Toolbars dialog box will appear.

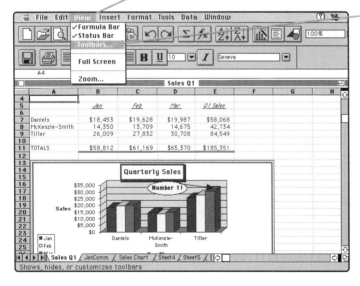

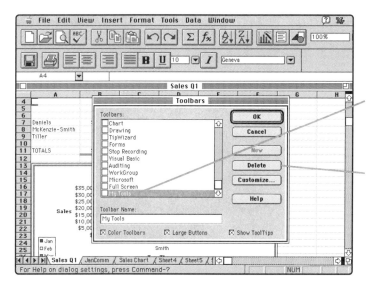

3. **Click** on the ⬇ to scroll down to My Tools at the bottom of the list box.

4. **Click** on **My Tools** to highlight it, and remove the ✗ from the box.

5. **Click** on **Delete**. A Microsoft Excel dialog box will appear.

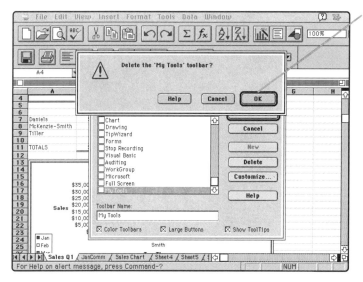

6. **Click** on **OK**. The Toolbar dialog box will appear in the foreground. The My Tools toolbar will disappear.

# RESTORING THE STANDARD AND FORMATTING TOOLBARS

1. **Click repeatedly** on the ⬆ to scroll up to the top of the toolbars list box.

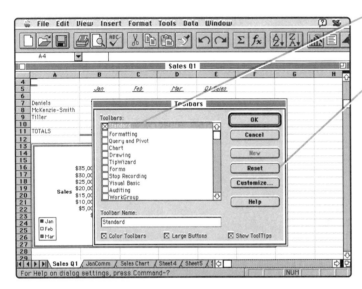

2. **Click** on **Standard** to highlight it, and place an ✕ in the box.

3. **Click** on **Reset**.

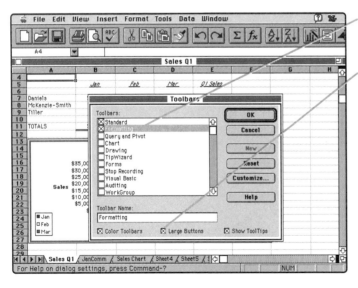

4. **Click** on **Formatting** to place an ✕ in the box.

5. **Click** on **Large buttons** to *remove* the ✕ from the box.

6. **Click** on **OK**. The Standard and Formatting toolbars will be restored with the original buttons and in their original size.

# Protecting Your Work

Excel offers many options in the way you can restrict access to a workbook or its contents. You can prevent others from opening or accessing a workbook. Or you can allow people to open your workbooks but prevent them from saving any changes. By using different passwords, you can even mix the kinds of protection you use in a single workbook so that different groups of people have different levels of access. Just make sure that you can remember each password (or write them down and file them in a safe place)! In this chapter, you will do the following:

❖ Assign password protection to a workbook
❖ Test a password
❖ Remove a password
❖ Assign a password to keep the original file intact
❖ Protect a single worksheet in a workbook
❖ Remove a password from a single worksheet

## ASSIGNING PASSWORD PROTECTION TO A WORKBOOK

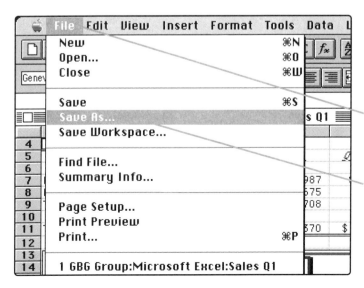

In this section, you will add a password to a workbook so that the workbook cannot be opened without it.

1. **Press and hold** on **File** in the menu bar. The pull-down menu will appear.

2. **Drag** the highlight bar to **Save As**, then **release** the mouse button. The Save As dialog box will appear.

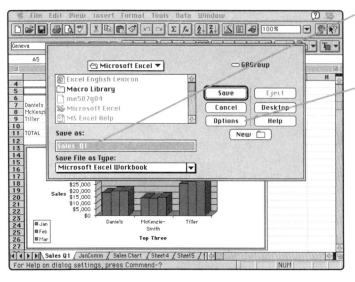

Confirm that the file you want to protect is listed in the Save As box.

3. **Click** on **Options**. The Save Options dialog box will appear.

4. **Type** a **password** in the **Protection Password box**. Each letter or number you type will show as an asterisk (*). A password can include as many as 15 characters in any combination. The password feature is case-sensitive, so if you use a combination of upper- and lowercase letters, you must remember the exact combination.

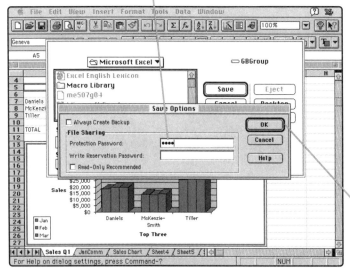

WARNING: If you forget your password, you are in deep fertilizer! You will have to re-create the entire file.

5. **Click** on **OK**. The Confirm Password dialog box will appear.

6. **Type** the **same password** in the **Reenter Protection Password box**.

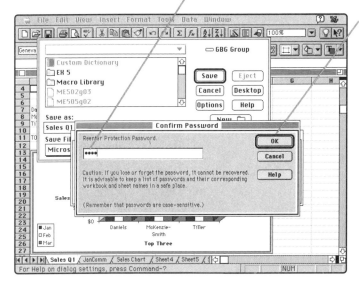

7. **Click** on **OK**. The Confirm Password dialog box will disappear and the Save As dialog box will come to the front.

8. **Click** on **Save** in the **Save As dialog box**. A Microsoft Excel message box will appear.

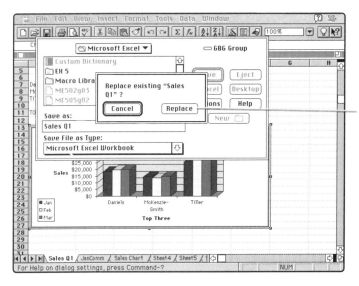

Excel asks if you want to replace the existing file with the one you have just protected with a password.

9. **Click** on **Replace**. The Microsoft Excel dialog box will disappear.

# TESTING A PASSWORD

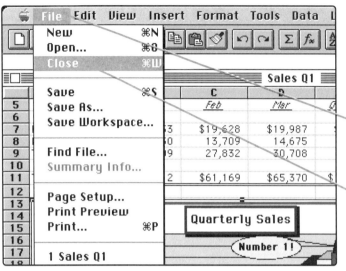

To test whether the password option will prevent unauthorized opening of the workbook, you must close the file and reopen it.

1. **Press and hold** on **File** in the menu bar. A pull-down menu will appear.

2. **Drag** the highlight bar to **Close**, then **release** the mouse button. The Sales Q1 file will close and an empty Excel screen will appear.

3. **Press and hold** on **File** in the menu bar. A pull-down menu will appear.

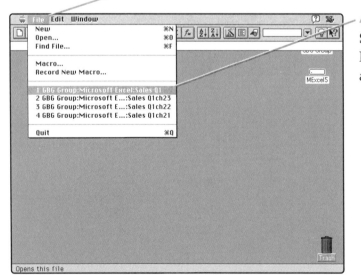

4. **Drag** the highlight bar to **Sales Q1** to open the file. The Password dialog box will appear.

5. **Type** the **password** in the **Password text box**.

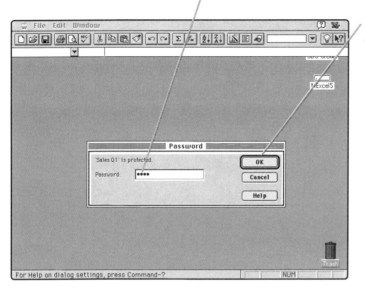

6. **Click** on **OK**. The Sales Q1 worksheet will appear.

## REMOVING A PASSWORD

In this section, you will delete the password you added to the workbook in the previous section.

1. **Press and hold** on **File** in the menu bar. A pull-down menu will appear.

2. **Drag** the highlight bar to **Save As**, then **release** the mouse button. The Save as dialog box will appear.

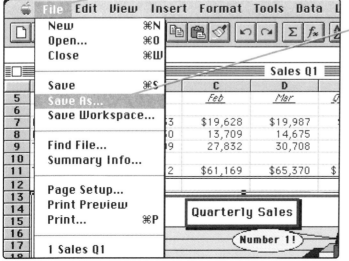

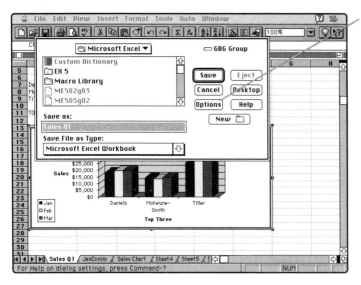

3. **Click** on **Options**. The Save Options dialog box will appear.

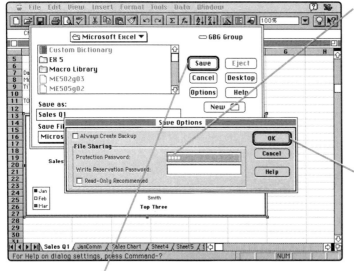

4. **Click twice** in the **Protection Password box** to highlight the field if it is not already highlighted.

5. **Press** the **Delete key** on your keyboard to remove the password.

6. **Click** on **OK**. The Save Options dialog box will disappear and the Save As dialog box will come to the front.

7. **Click** on **Save** in the Save As dialog box. A Microsoft Excel message box will appear.

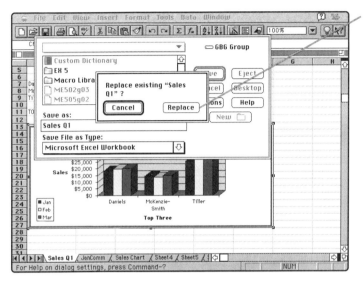

8. **Click** on **Replace**. The Sales Q1 worksheet will appear.

## ASSIGNING A PASSWORD TO KEEP THE ORIGINAL FILE INTACT

1. **Repeat steps 1 through 3** in the section "Assigning Password Protection to a Workbook" at the beginning of this chapter to open the Save Options dialog box.

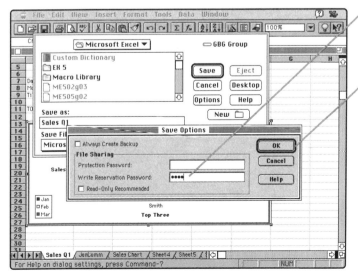

2. **Click** on the **Write Reservation Password box** and **type** a **password**.

3. **Click** on **OK**. The Confirm Password dialog box will appear.

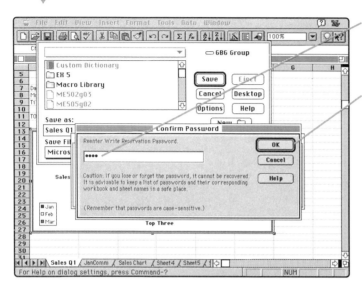

4. **Type** the **same password** in the **Reenter Write Reservation dialog box**.

5. **Click** on **OK**. The Confirm Password dialog box will disappear.

6. **Click** on **Save** in the **Save As dialog box**. A Microsoft Excel message box will appear.

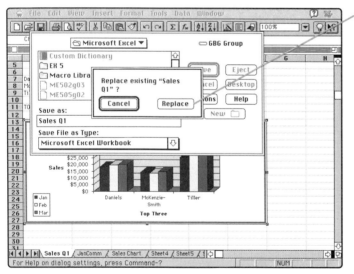

7. **Click** on **Replace**. The Microsoft Excel dialog box will disappear.

# PROTECTING A SINGLE WORKSHEET IN A WORKBOOK

You can allow a person to open a workbook but prevent him or her from making changes in a specific worksheet without the correct password.

1. **Press and hold** on **Tools** in the menu bar. A pull-down menu will appear.

2. **Drag** the highlight bar to **Protection**. A second menu will appear.

3. **Drag** the highlight bar to **Protect Sheet**, then **release** the mouse button. The Protect Sheet dialog box will appear.

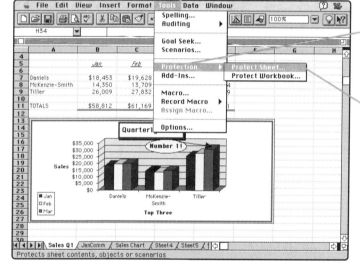

Notice that an × appears in the squares to the left of "Contents," "Objects," and "Scenarios." Excel has already selected all of the items to be protected. To customize the levels of protection, refer to your *Users Guide*.

4. **Type** a **password** in the **Password text box**.

5. **Click** on **OK**. A Confirm Password dialog box will appear.

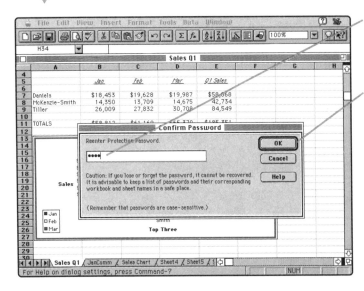

6. **Type** the **same password** in the **Reenter Protection Password dialog box**.

7. **Click** on **OK**. The Sales Q1 file with password-protected worksheets will appear in the window.

## REMOVING PASSWORD PROTECTION FROM A WORKSHEET

1. **Press and hold** on **Tools** in the menu bar. A pull-down menu will appear.

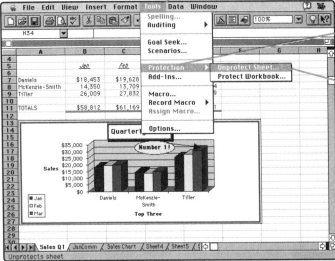

2. **Drag** the highlight bar to **Protection**. A side bar will appear.

3. **Drag** the highlight bar to **Unprotect Worksheet**, then **release** the mouse button. An Unprotect Sheet dialog box will appear.

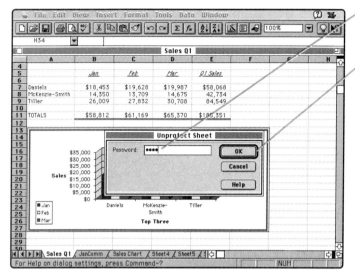

4. **Type** the **password** that protects the sheet.

5. **Click** on **OK**. The dialog box disappears and the sheet is now unprotected.

# CHAPTER 27

# Converting Another Program's Worksheet to Excel

If the file you want to convert has been created in a Windows version of a program, and you have an exchange program installed such as PC Exchange or Apple File Exchange, your Macintosh will read the PC disk directly. If you don't have an exchange program, you will need to convert the file to Macintosh using a conversion program such as Mac-to-DOS. In this chapter you will do the following:

❖ Open a worksheet from Excel 4 for Windows and convert it to an Excel 5 for the Macintosh worksheet.

❖ Make formatting changes to the converted spreadsheet.

❖ Save the converted worksheet as an Excel 5 for the Macintosh file.

## OPENING A WORKSHEET FROM ANOTHER PROGRAM

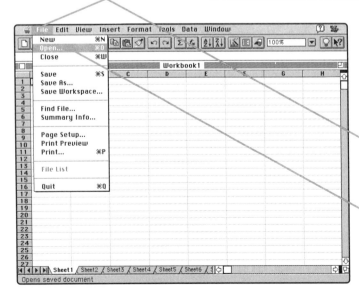

Have the file you want to convert copied into the Microsoft Excel folder on your hard drive. Excel 5 should be open.

1. **Press and hold** on **File** in the menu bar. A pull-down menu will appear.

2. **Drag** the highlight bar to **Open**, then **release** the mouse button. The Open File dialog box will appear.

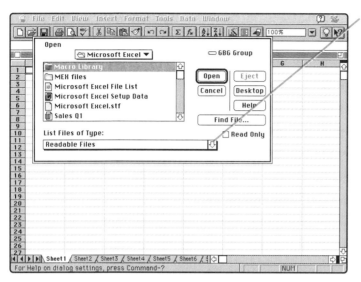

3. **Press and hold** on the ↓ on the File text box. A drop-down list of file types will appear.

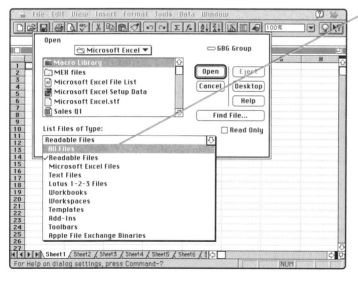

4. **Drag** the highlight bar to the **type of file** you want to convert, then release the mouse button. It will appear in the file type text box. In this example, we are using All Files.

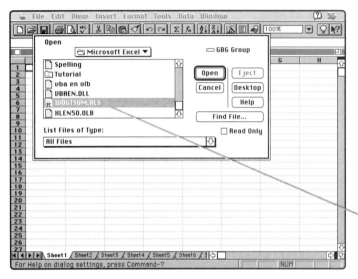

Notice that the list of files in the Microsoft Excel folder has changed.

5. **Click repeatedly** on the ⬇ to scroll down the list of files until you find the worksheet you want to convert. In this example, the file is the WDGTSUM.XLS.

6. **Click twice** on the **file** you want to convert. The file will open.

# ADDING SPREADSHEET GRIDLINES

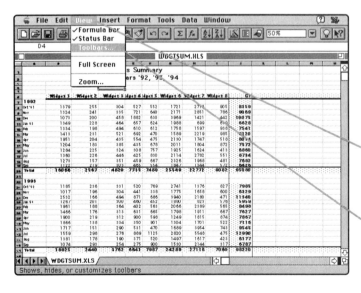

Your spreadsheet may not have all the formatting or formulas still applied when you open it into Excel. If the gridlines don't appear, do the following steps:

1. **Press and hold** on **View** in the menu bar. A pull-down menu will appear.

2. **Drag** the highlight bar to **Toolbars**, then **release** the mouse button. The Toolbars dialog box will appear.

3. **Click** on **Forms** to put an ✕ in the box.

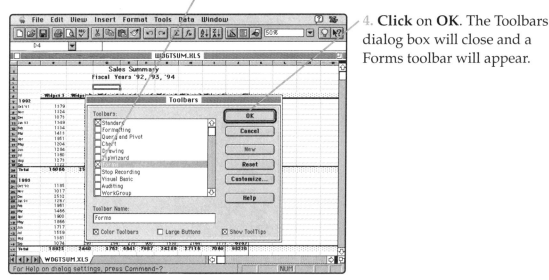

4. **Click** on **OK**. The Toolbars dialog box will close and a Forms toolbar will appear.

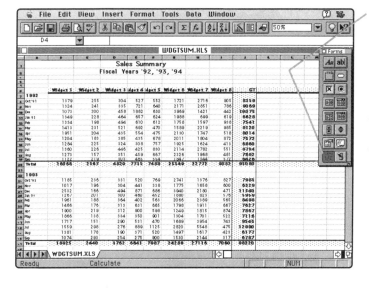

5. **Click** on the **Toggle Grid button** at the bottom left of the toolbar. After a pause the gridlines will disappear.

6. **Click** on the **Toggle Grid button** again to turn the gridlines off and on.

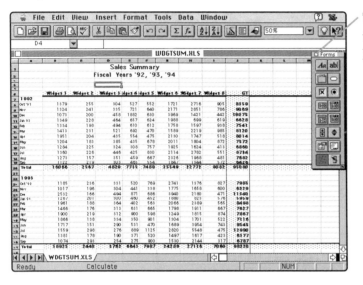

7. **Click** on the **Close box** on the Forms toolbar to close the Forms toolbar.

# SAVING A CONVERTED FILE AS AN EXCEL WORKBOOK FILE

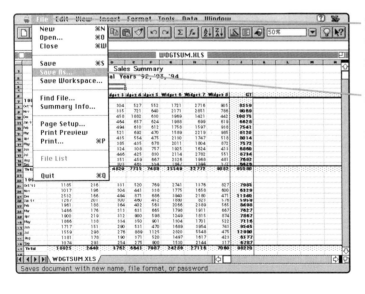

1. **Press and hold** on **File** in the menu bar. A pull-down menu will appear.

2. **Drag** the highlight bar to **Save As**, then **release** the mouse button.

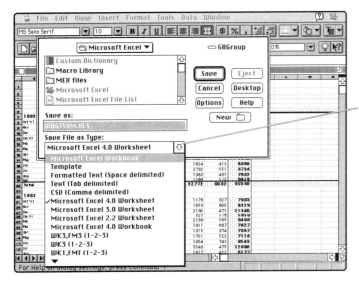

Notice that the Microsoft Excel 4.0 file format is selected in the Save File as Type box.

3. **Press and hold** on the ⬇ next to the Save File as Type box. A drop down list will appear.

4. **Drag** the highlight bar up or down the list until you see **Microsoft Excel Workbook**, then **release** the mouse button.

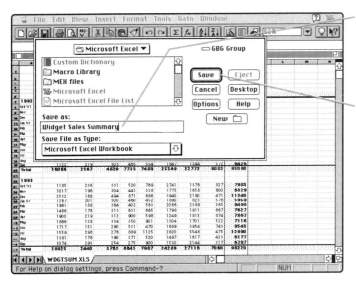

5. **Type "Widget Sales Summary"** to replace "WDGTSUM.XLS" in the Save As box.

6. **Click** on **Save**. You will see the Summary Info dialog box. See "Naming a Workbook" in Chapter 2, if you need help with this dialog box.

The Save As command creates a new Excel 5 file and leaves the original file unchanged.

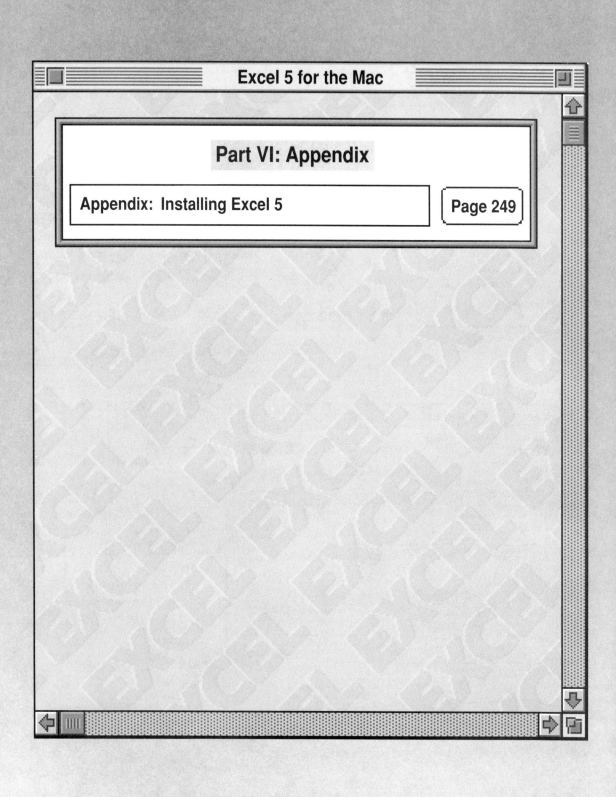

Excel 5 for the Mac

# Part VI: Appendix

Appendix: Installing Excel 5

Page 249

# Installing Excel 5

This appendix will describe a standard (typical) first-time installation for Excel 5. You can also do these steps if you are upgrading to Excel 5. In both instances, however, the installation program will interact with your particular computer. Therefore, you may see slightly different screens or messages than shown in these examples. If you want to customize your installation, refer to the *User's Guide* that came with your software. In this appendix, you will do the following:

❖ Install Excel 5

Before you start, make sure that you have made and are using backup copies of your Excel 5 Install disks. If you need help backing up your disks, see the *User's Guide*.

## INSTALLING EXCEL 5 FOR THE MACINTOSH

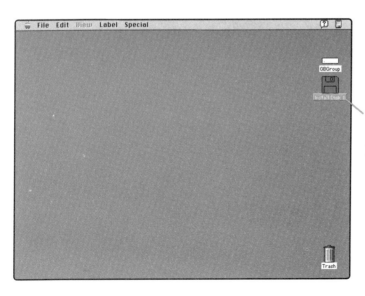

1. **Insert** your backup copy of **Excel 5 Install Disk 1**. The Install Disk 1 icon will appear on the desktop.

2. **Click twice** on the **Install Disk 1 icon**. The Install Disk 1 Folder will appear.

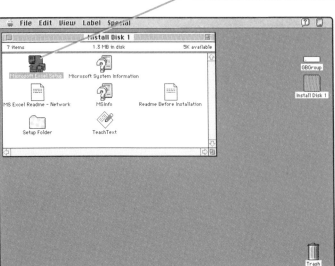

3. **Click twice** on the **Microsoft Excel Setup icon**. After a pause, the Microsoft Excel 5.0 setup dialog box will appear.

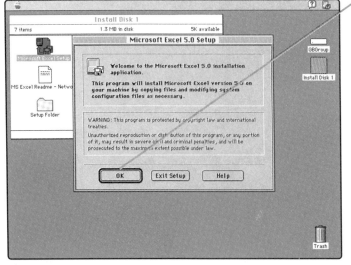

4. **Click** on **OK.** The Name and Organization Information box will appear.

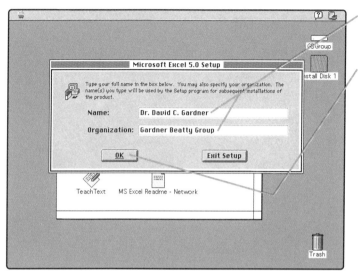

5. **Type your name** and **organization name.**

6. **Click** on **OK**. The Name Confirmation box will appear.

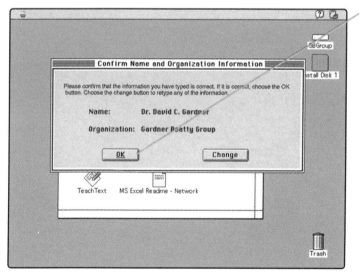

7. If your name and organization appear correctly, **click** on **OK**. If your name and organization name are not correct, **click** on **Change** and repeat steps 5 through 6. A product identification dialog box will appear.

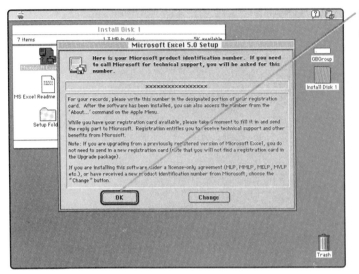

**8. Click** on **OK.** A Destination dialog box will appear.

Notice that Microsoft Excel 5 automatically created and named its own folder on your hard drive.

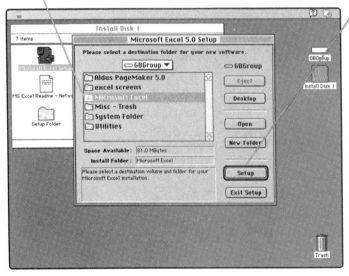

**8. Click** on **Setup.** The Install Type dialog box will appear.

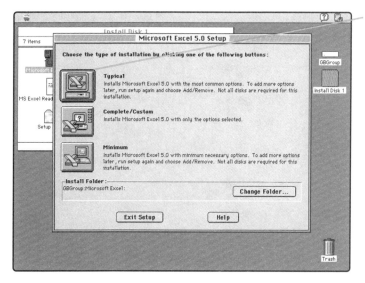

9. **Click** on **Typical.** A Microsoft Excel 5.0 Setup message box will appear.

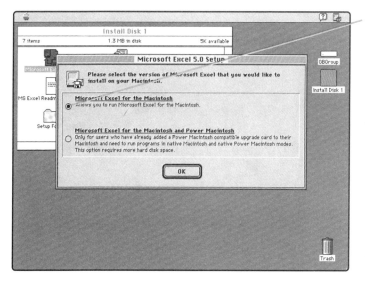

10. **Click** on the **appropriate statement** to place a dot in the circle. In this example, it is "Microsoft Excel for the Macintosh."

11. **Click** on **OK.**

**Note:** If you are installing on a Power Macintosh, you will have a third option on your screen. Click on the "Microsoft Excel for the Power Macintosh" option.

At this point sit back and relax. Excel will now begin copying the files from the disks to your hard drive.

The Microsoft Excel 5.0 dialog box will show you the percentage of completion in copying files.

When Excel has copied all the files from that disk, it will automatically eject the disk and the message box will request that the next disk in the series be inserted.

**12. Insert** the rest of the disks when prompted.

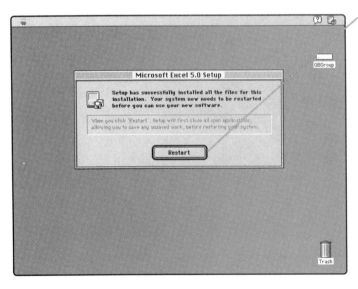

Congratulations! You have successfully installed Excel 5.0.

**13. Click** on **Restart**. Your Mac will restart and you will be back at the original desktop.

Now you're ready to go to Chapter 1 to learn how to open Excel.

# Index